THE ULTIMATE KID

Levels of Learning That Make a Difference
by Jeffrey Goelitz

University of the Trees Press
P.O. Box 66
Boulder Creek, CA. 95006

Cover design by Mary Michaels
Cover photography by Barbara Oberg
Cover model is Ursula Oberg

Printed in the United States by Arcata Graphics

ISBN: 0-916438-61-9

Acknowledgements

There are many dear people who helped bring *The Ultimate Kid* into print. Their caring and constructive criticism have greatly improved the book's quality.

I am thankful to Dr. Christopher Hills and Dr. Deborah Rozman whose joint creation, *Exploring Inner Space*, acted as a model for the content and format. Their insight into human nature has left a deep impression on me.

My good friend, Judy Gold, was of great help also. From her many years of innovative teaching in public school, she has developed a repertoire of skills which she so generously contributed to my efforts. Judy was my sounding board on countless ideas. She recharged me with vision when I struggled. A special thanks goes also to Robert Baretta-Lorton (author of *Mathematics...A Way of Thinking*, Addison-Wesley, 1977). His creativity and understanding of how children learn has greatly inspired me.

I am indebted to the editors, Ann Ray and Euphrasia Carroll, for their patient work in the book's refinement. I am thankful to Kathie Dunham who worked many long hours typing and Cheryll Melott whose devoted care and thoroughness with final proof reading, organization, form and documentation brought *The Ultimate Kid* to its completion. I want to also acknowledge the efforts of the photographers, Sheila Carrillo and Barbara Oberg.

Finally, I am grateful to the many children who gave me much inspiration. Through them my life is a hundred times richer.

Table of Contents

The Ultimate Kid

Introduction

When I look at children, I see their whole being. It is almost as though I'm seeing through a large plate glass window into the privacy of their home. Everything is showing: their character, strength, flaws, self-concept, even their motivations. I clear my mind of the moment's preoccupations or thoughts and immediately I'm experiencing what it's like to be that child. This isn't a great skill. Children themselves do it all the time. It's easy for them because they are not carrying around a lot of excess mental baggage to color their perceptions.

Let me show you what I mean by inviting you into my class. It is a Monday afternoon, and I'm trying to teach an African geography lesson according to my schedule which is rigorous and fast-paced. The information on the main exports of Western Africa must be communicated, because if it isn't, then we might run out of time for the lesson on the main exports of Eastern Africa.

While I am sharing the material a tall lanky boy in the corner of my classroom is fidgeting with his pencil, anxiously waiting for class to finish so he can go to P.E. and passionately play his great love, basketball. He is only partially present when I talk about the exports of peanuts, cacao, and palm oil. I feel some empathy inside because I know what he is feeling. Basketball was also my own great passion. When I was in school it was a real source of pride for me because I was good at it. I could jump high, shoot well, and dribble the ball like a superstar. When it came to classwork, I felt more like a klutz. So here is this boy in the corner of the room, with a basketball physique if there ever was one, and he's dying to gain back some of the self-respect that during the school day has been eroded in class. No wonder he can never get the facts straight on African geography.

Another uneasy student is Peter. He is a very intelligent and likeable boy with a caring heart. He's very conscientious and tries to do what is fair and right. At the same time he can be his own worst enemy. He has a very fragile part of himself, a feeling of low self-worth that can trigger an explosive temper and even make him pick a fight with someone twice his size. Despite being an excellent student, Peter sometimes doesn't like himself and compares himself unfavorably with others. He would gladly trade his smarts for a below-average intelligence with an athletic body and a lively personality. I realized that any academic skills or challenges I passed on to Peter would pale in comparison to the need for him to feel good about himself. Somehow, in addition to the subject matter, I had to instill some self-confidence in Peter. Otherwise he might carry this burden of poor self-worth for the rest of his life.

Like all of us, the basketball player and Peter have areas of strength and weakness. They'll continue to do well in their area of strength because they're naturally talented and motivated in those areas. That leaves the trouble spots. Those are the squeaky wheels that need special attention. Left to themselves, these flaws in character or gaps in intelligence will continue to undermine a person's creative contribution to life. Parents and teachers frequently don't recognize these subtleties or, if they do, they don't know what to do about it. Fortunately, we have some new models of education that are a great help in making children whole. Many theories from recent brain research are being brought into practical application both in the home and in the classroom. Loosely called "Whole Brain Learning", these new techniques of teaching are exciting because they offer effective, alternative ways to educate children. This doesn't mean doing away with traditional teaching methods, textbooks, or worksheets, which are a strong and essential part of education. It means that: (1) there are other ways to present material to children, ways that are imaginative and personally engrossing and (2) there are areas of need in children which must be addressed in order for their lives to be richer and more fulfilling. Pretend for a moment that you are a child hearing about the famous Boston Tea Party for the first time. But instead of reading the sequence of events in a U.S. History book, you're going to be led through a visualization or guided imagery with your eyes closed. In your imagination you will actually experience the event as if you were there witnessing the action live. For example:

On December 16th, 1773, you and a group of colonists are disguised as Indians. Quietly you walk along together and you do not even whisper. You board three British tea ships in the Boston Harbor. The night air is cold and the atmosphere scary because British troops are nearby. You could be in great danger if caught. As you begin dumping what will be 340 chests of tea into the harbor, you realize the importance of the event. You are defying the British authorities and their demand for tax on imported tea. In effect you are saying, "I want to control what happens in my own government. I want democracy. No outside authority is going to tell me what to do." There is an equal mixture of excitement and fear among you and the other rebels: excitement about creating something new and yet fear at the danger involved. The experience is very real for you. It is not an experience you will soon forget. You were there!

Visualization is one example of a new learning tool that has tremendous educational value. Think back for a second to the basketball player whose recall of verbal and written information is very poor. By using his imagination to fantasize on African geography instead of fantasizing about basketball, we're tapping areas of his natural intelligence that before were going to waste. I use visualization all the time in my classes because first of all, it's fun, and second of all, the kids don't forget those images. The experience is much more alive for them than a lecture or reading from a textbook; this is why visualization, as a teaching device, has the power to improve memory, to stimulate creative thinking, and to keep kids excited about learning. This is only one of many techniques to receive the much-needed support of modern brain research.

Much of the brain research in the last fifteen years indirectly ties in to what thinkers promoting human potential have been saying for centuries-that we greatly under use the capacity of our brain. If you think about your average day you'll probably agree. So much is routine, predictable, and lacking in challenge or creativity. We tend to lean towards the secure and familiar instead of going towards the unknown where we might discover something new in life. It is not surprising that some scientists speculate that we use only ten percent of our brain and that our higher creative intelligence remains untapped most of the time.

Let's look at several of the brain theories which are opening up new doors in education and child-raising and are making us re-examine what it is to be human and how we learn. Of particular interest to educators and psychologists are the popular right brain/left brain theory, the Triune model, and the recent work of Dr. Christopher Hills' theory of the Seven-Tiered Brain. The work of Dr. Hills is the primary inspiration for this book.

LEFT AND RIGHT BRAIN FUNCTION

Consider first the left brain/right brain theory which states that each half of our split-hemisphere brain has unique functions which predominate in specific types of activities. According to this theory, the left brain specializes in verbal, analytic types of activity while the right brain is more efficient at visual-spatial tasks, seeing images, and activities of a feeling type.

Left Brain	Right Brain
verbal	non-verbal
recognizes parts	recognizes wholes
logical	intuitive/emotional
step-by-step	simultaneous
good at naming and understanding words	forms visual images

When this theory first came out, there was a lot of excitement about its far reaching implications on the way the brain worked and how we learn. More recently the left brain/right brain theory is thought to be oversimplified. Overall research with brain damaged children and use of the EEG (electro-encephalograph) machine to determine the brain's hemispheric preference of one type of activity over another is inconclusive. While certain human functions do appear to be localized in either the left or right hemisphere, this is not necessarily an innate physical capability but perhaps more of an acquired trait. Experiments with brain damaged children have demonstrated that one side of the brain can be taught an activity that according to the left brain/right brain theory is supposed to be under the elite control of the other side of the brain. One of the great contributions of the split brain theory has been the insight that we must use our whole brain to become the best learners we can be. The approach to learning in our society concentrates more on the verbal, analytic part of the brain, but the left brain/right brain model makes very clear the idea that one hemisphere is not necessarily better than the other and that in fact, creative thinking requires both.

THE TRIUNE BRAIN MODEL

The Triune Brain model developed by Dr. Paul Maclean states that we have three layers in our brain which grew in stages over our evolutionary past. Each brain has a different function that will predominate depending on the life situation which faces us. The Reptilean brain is the oldest brain and is responsible for bodily controls like breathing and digestion as well as basic survival needs. The Reptilean brain learns through imitation and ritual. The Limbic brain is sometimes called the emotional brain and follows stimulus-response, reward-punishment type of learning. The top and most recently developed brain is called the Neo-Cortex brain. Higher human intelligence resides in the Neo-Cortex. Inspiration and creativity motivate this thinking type of brain. We can see from the Triune model that each one of the brains has a unique role to play in learning. The exclusion of any one brain, especially the Neo-Cortex brain, can limit a person's capacity to learn.

THE SEVEN-TIERED BRAIN

When we come to Christopher Hills' Seven-Tiered Brain system, we are dealing with a comprehensive, far-reaching brain theory that goes farther than the right brain/left brain theory and the Triune model in understanding human behavior. Dr. Hills' theory states that the human brain has seven major faculties, each with a specialized function or mode of learning. These seven domains of the brain have evolved through millions of years of time. The concept of the Seven-Tiered Brain model can be seen in the diagram below.

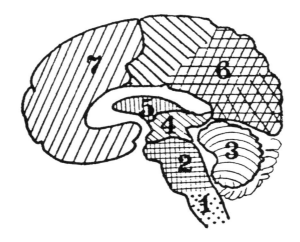

Physical Faculty of the Brain	Learning Function Associated With Each Part of the Brain
1. Medulla Oblongata	Physical Expression/Senses
2. Pons	Social Life
3. Cerebellum	Intellect
4. Mid-brain	Sense of Security/Emotions
5. Inter-brain, Third Ventricle	Conceptual Mind
6. Occipital, Parietal & Temporal Lobes	Intuition/Sensitivity
7. Frontal Lobes	Imagination

Initially it may be difficult to see how such abstruse theories apply to the education of children. How can these models possibly be of any interest to a budding young basketball star or to a sad-hearted child like Peter?

Let's take the Seven-Tiered Brain model as an example. To practically appreciate this theory, look at the following scenario:

Suppose I ask four nine-year-olds to build a bookcase from scratch. All the materials are to be supplied ahead of time including wood of various sizes, saws, rulers and tape measures, nails, hammers, pencils and plain paper. The only thing missing is any kind of instruction whatsoever. Now let the children begin.

The approaches to the project vary tremendously. One boy immediately begins hammering wood together in a frenzy. All planning is thrown out the window in the rush to physically finish first. Result? - a functionless, dilapidated mess. Another boy slyly waits like a fox, eyeing the approaches and results of others. He keeps what is useful in their methods and dispenses with the rest. Nothing original arises from this boy and his level of fulfillment is as mediocre as his manifestation. Nevertheless, he creates a bookshelf that, although unoriginal, is functional. Meanwhile, a girl off in a corner is still held up at the idea level. Six pages of plans from pencil and ruler account for her time. Each plan represents a revision of the previous one. At this rate, she'll never lift a hammer.

There is only one child that is meeting the challenge successfully. This boy just closes his eyes and visualizes several designs which he then sketches onto paper. He quickly inspects the work of the other children to possibly integrate any good ideas into his plans, and he makes sure that his supplies and building materials are adequate to complete his design. The detailed plan for the bookshelf follows as he takes exact measurements, and the final step is the actual creation: a well thought out original and functional bookshelf.

The first boy was operating almost entirely at the physical level. The girl was operating from the intellect, totally omitting the physical level. Only the fourth child that I described feels really good within himself because he has harnessed as much of his full creativity and intelligence as possible.

In working with children as a teacher for the past ten years, I have noticed how much of their ability to learn or even their ability to be happy is dependent upon the development of different levels of their consciousness. This is why I feel so strongly the need for an education that deals with all levels of learning. Many academically high-achieving children are uncomfortable in their social relations; they feel awkward and uncommunicative in the company of others. "Street-wise" kids are unable to trust other children or adults and they put too much of their attention on troublesome relationships rather than academics. Bright children become bored because their minds aren't challenged. To me, it is very clear that if these needs are not dealt with somewhere along the line, they will probably accompany these children into adulthood.

The Ultimate Kid strives to respond to children's needs and to teach all levels of their being. It recognizes that children not only need to excel in academics but also need to learn how to express and understand feelings, develop social skills, listen to the guiding voice of their own intuition, and enjoy the creativity of an open imagination.

Recently I watched a boy playing with a stick in a local river. I watched him hurl the four-foot-long harpoon into a make-believe fish. Then the stick became a submarine. Skillfully it maneuvered underneath and around potentially dangerous enemy ships. A few times it took some minor hits on its side from nearby warships, but the boy Commander quickly navigated it out of danger. Then the boy's creativity set to work again, and all of a sudden a great race developed between the stick and other competing sticks as the boy simultaneously pushed one stick with his right hand and another stick with his left. The first stick to cross the finish line would be the winner, and a dozen sticks of all sizes and shapes were competing in a tremendous splashing of water. The winner became the boy's special scepter while the losers, still floating in the river, were pelted by pebbles.

As I stood watching, the boy created magic games, and then went hunting wild animals and was just beginning a war fantasy when his mother, from some fifty yards down the beach, called out that it was time for them to go home. As the boy left, I felt a great sense of joy. "My God," I thought, "what creativity that boy has!" It was like observing a symphony of imagination in action.

In many of our schools or homes, this richness of expression might go totally unappreciated. The boy's worth would be determined by the number of multiplication tables he does in ten minutes or by his spelling test scores. In fact, his imaginative world might be condemned as fanciful and useless rather than acknowledged as a potential area of intelligence that needs to be coordinated with all his levels of being. This is a challenge for teachers and parents. We need to recognize the learning potential in children and draw it out in its full splendor. The sad thing is that, without training in all seven areas of brain development, some wonderful aspect of a child's personality or expression is almost sure to remain underdeveloped. I'm talking about an ultimate education here, not a pie-in-the-sky, theorist's approach to the daily education that goes on in the classroom or home. All the activities in this book, which are organized around the Seven-Tiered Brain theory, have been successfully used in school classrooms, in homes and also in adult settings. Given the demands on educators and parents these days to buckle down to basics, improve test scores, and raise academic standards, *The Ultimate Kid* offers new ways of learning that enhance performance for all of these requirements. Instead of working with only select parts of the brain, activities are presented that tap the whole brain potential.

The idea for writing this book originally came from a book called *Exploring Inner Space* by Christopher Hills and Deborah Rozman. Many of the activities from that book have been adapted for this text, but whereas that book was designed for all age groups, *The Ultimate Kid* speaks primarily to the needs of children. It recognizes the fact that teachers and parents are very busy these days; hence a simple, straight-forward format has been presented that doesn't require a lot of reading or figuring out. The book is divided into seven chapters, each chapter containing activities from one of the seven domains of learning. In many cases, activities will incorporate more than one mode of learning.

It has been a great joy writing this book and an even bigger joy practicing these activities with children over the last six years. We have shared many tender and powerful moments. And while these children are undoubtedly still meeting the challenge of overcoming self-limitations, new doors of seeing and experiencing have opened up in many of them. For me it's always a new and inspiring moment and always special to watch that unfolding of a child's potential. I hope you'll use this book to help create these moments of unfoldment with your own children.

Jeffrey Goelitz

Boulder Creek, CA.

Summer 1986

Chapter 1

PHYSICAL EXPRESSION/SENSES

Physical Expression/Senses

Children grow up in the physical world of the senses. It is their predominant way of experiencing life. They put things in their mouths. They desire to touch every object they come in contact with. Because children haven't lived a long time yet, they haven't accumulated many concepts through their experience. When the mind develops, the focus of the senses diminishes. Memory begins to color children's experience. When eating an apple, the image of an apple creeps in subconsciously so that we're eating a concept or memory as much as we're eating an apple. Or the mind thinks of other thoughts or preoccupations while the mouth eats. The vibrant, sensory moment is blurred by the activated mind.

It is important that children don't lose the vital awareness of their senses. The full use of the senses makes the experience in life so much richer and fuller. Experiencing the physical world also means exploring the body and the objects in the surrounding environment. What an unusual and gifted instrument the body is! It is as if children gradually wake up from a dream to find themselves with this body that they can move around like a puppet.

Blindwalk

We strongly rely on our sense of sight to familiarize ourselves and to interpret the world around us. Yet many blind people lead fulfilled and creative lives despite the lack of sight. These people, including modern musicians like Stevie Wonder, Ray Charles, and Jose' Feliciano, have substituted a heightened awareness and application of their other senses for the use of their eyes. A blindwalk acquaints children with the potential abilities of the nonvisual senses plus develops a feeling of trust and caring between the participants.

Goal:

1. To more fully experience and appreciate the nonvisual senses.

2. To develop trust and caring with a partner.

Preparation:

1. A blindfold for every pair of partners.

2. Chalkboard/chalk or poster board/marker.

Procedure:

1. Tell the children that they're going to do a blindwalk outdoors (or, if suitable, indoors). Everyone will be working in pairs, with one person leading and the other person being led while blindfolded. Emphasize the trust part of the activity; the guide must carefully lead his/her partner around safely. With younger children either pair them up with an adult or allow them to be guided by other young children only under closely monitored circumstances and in a spacious area. The goal of this activity is to more fully experience the physical world and its many textures, smells, sounds, and impressions.

2. Divide the group into pairs and hand out a blindfold to each pair.

3. Instruct the pairs to go outside and then begin the activity within carefully marked boundaries. After ten minutes, have the partners switch roles.

4. When the children are finished have them come back inside and sit down with their eyes closed. Ask them to relive the blindfolded experience. What was it like? Did it feel safe and comfortable? What senses did they experience differently?

5. Now divide the children into three groups-textures, sounds, and smells. Ask each respective group which textures, sounds, or smells they experienced. Record their answers on a chalkboard or poster board.

6. On another day lead the children in a blindwalk again but this time in a totally different environment like a library, gymnasium, forest, etc. Ask the same questions afterwards and see if their experiences with texture, sound, and smell differ from the previous blindwalk held in a different environment.

Touch the Earth

Touch the Earth is a simple, fun exercise that children enjoy because it is physically and mentally challenging. Similar to the game of "Simon Says", the supervising adult gives instructions to the children on specific physical positions to take. The positions begin to change quickly and only the most alert listeners can follow the rapid and sometimes deliberately confusing instructions. The result is a lot of laughter, excitement, and robust physical exercise.

"Touch the Earth"

"Touch the Mountains"

Area: Physical Movement, Listening Skills   **Skill Level:** Grades K-8

Goals: 1.   To exercise and stretch the body.

                      2.   To improve listening skills.

Preparation: Make sure that the children have an arm's length of space around themselves to allow for stationary movement.

Procedure: 1.   Demonstrate the five different physical positions in *Touch the Earth.* (See pictures on the previous and following page.) Begin with a normal standing position with legs together and arms to the side. "Touch the Sky" is raising one's arms and hands in the air as high as possible. "Touch a Tree" is extending one's arms sideways parallel to the floor. "Touch the Mountains" is placing one's hands on the hips. "Touch the Earth" is lowering the arms to the floor with the back as straight as possible. And finally "Over the Waterfalls" is extending the arms over the back with the back in an arched position.

                      2.   Explain to the children that *Touch the Earth* is like "Simon Says" except that there are two parts. In the first part the leader calls out a position and then moves into the position. Everyone in turn follows the movement of the leader. Tell the children that the speed of the instructions may vary and it will be challenging for some of the children to keep up. Part two of this activity becomes much more challenging because it involves trickery. The children are to listen to the verbal instructions only, ignoring whatever physical positions the leader demonstrates. In other words, the leader might call, "Touch the Sky!" but be in a "Touch the Tree" position. The children should be in the "Touch the Sky" position or what the leader called out. Again, vary the speed.

"Touch the Trees"

"Over the Waterfalls"

"Touch the Sky"

Five Senses Visualization

Our happiness is frequently related to the information we receive through our senses. The bright, warm sun makes us cheerful. Some music will delight us, other music will annoy us. Seeing our good friend playing with another friend can make us feel joyful while at other times the same experience creates insecurity. A hot and tasty meal makes us feel secure and content. Hearing of a friend injured in an accident can sadden us. But what would it be like without our senses? How would we experience life? The following activity, which takes us on a journey beyond the senses, is a wonderful opportunity for children to experience a deeper part of themselves.

Goal:

1. To appreciate the senses.

2. To deepen awareness of ourselves.

Procedure:

1. Talk about the senses with the group and what the senses do for us. Discuss how certain people (blind, deaf) still live very fulfilling lives without use of one or more senses. Tell the children that they are going to experience briefly what it would be like to be without some or all of the senses.

2. Prepare the children for a quiet visualization by having them first relax their bodies, either through short stretching exercises, or by tensing and relaxing each body part in turn. Then, ask the children to take several deep inhalations and exhalations.

3. Begin the visualization by asking the children to close their eyes. Now, in a soft and soothing voice, say the following with pauses between each sentence:

"Pretend that you've never seen anything before. You've never seen color, people, sunshine, trees. Try to imagine what it is like to be blind...How do you sense the world around you?..Now, imagine that you've never heard anything before. From birth, you've been blind and deaf. You've never heard voices or sounds...How do you sense the world around you?.. Now let's take away the sense of touch...You can't feel anything: pleasure or pain...How would you know what space is or what objects are in space without the sense of touch? All you have left are the senses of smell and taste...Now, let's remove the sense of smell...You've never smelled pizza or flowers or perfume...What is it like to be unable to smell? Now, let's take away the last sense remaining, the sense of taste...You've never tasted anything, neither food, nor toothpaste nor the taste of your mouth. What is left now? Just your awareness...Let's gradually bring the senses back, one by one. Bring back the sense of taste...Now bring back the sense of smell, drawing in the air gently...Next return the sense of touch to your awareness, feeling the weight of your body...Now, add the sense of hearing, listening to the sounds in the room...Finally, bring back the sense of sight by opening your eyes."

4. Discuss with the children what they experienced. Ask them what sense was most difficult to leave behind. What sense was easiest to leave behind? Finally, ask them what was left when all the senses were removed.

Banquet for the Senses

During this activity the children are going to re-experience what it's like to be a baby on a sensory level. Blindfolded, everyone will be led through a feast of various sense experiences. By being blindfolded, their mental prejudgements and memories of experiences are cut off so they live entirely in the moment. Kids love the unpredictable spontaneity of these exercises which you can see by looking at their expressive faces.

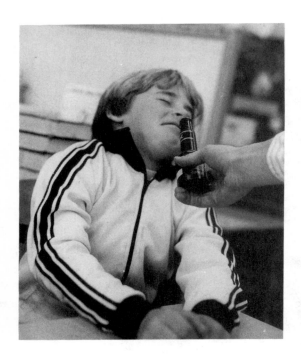

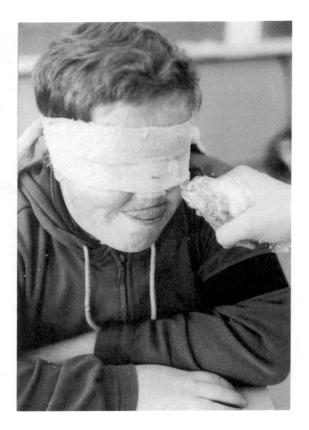

Area: Sense Awareness

Goal:

1. To become more aware of the senses, deepening sensitivity to each one.

Preparation:

1. Blindfolds for everyone.

2. Dishes, plates, paper cups to hold different objects and foods.

3. At least four different sources of smell (spices, flowers, colognes, plants, soaps, foods, etc.).

4. Four sources of taste (orange, lemon, onion, apple, cinnamon, honey, carob, salt, pepper, etc.).

5. Four sources of touch (a rough rock, smooth stone, waxy leaf, piece of cotton, fur or sponge, sandpaper, plastic, metal, velvet, etc.).

6. Four sources of sound (bell, woodblocks, sandpaper, whistle, gong, trickle of water poured from one bowl to another, etc.).

7. Napkins.

Procedure:

1. Hand out napkins to all children.

2. Have everyone blindfolded and request quiet in the room.

3. Begin by creating the different sources of sound, one by one.

4. Pass around the different objects of smell.

5. Next pass around, one at a time, the different objects collected for the sense of touch.

6. Pass around the plates that contain different items of taste, encouraging the children to use napkins if their hands get sticky.

7. Request that the children take off their blindfolds and be aware of the first thing that catches their visible attention.

8. Have the children share what they experienced. Ask them what sense they liked the most, which one they liked the least. Finally, ask them if being blindfolded helps them more fully experience their senses as compared to normal times.

Comments: Make sure that you keep all objects out of sight beforehand until you need them. Also, request that the children do not talk during this activity as their comments can influence and preempt another child's fresh experience. Circulate the objects quickly so that the children don't have to wait a long time until their next experience. An adult helper or mature child can speed up this process, especially with younger children.

Graphing

Graphing is a simple way of recording different bits of information. By using graph paper or even counting items like beads or buttons, we can represent data pictorially through symbols like X's or piles of multi-colored beads. From this information we can draw conclusions and see patterns in life. Often times we will ask children to make comparisons and see relationships between things. We cannot, however, expect children to give us insightful conclusions merely through abstract teaching, anymore than our taking a semester of Russian language will enable us to read the daily *Pravda* with good comprehension . For many children, learning through ideas, verbal or written, isn't as effective as learning through pictures or concrete representations of ideas. That's why graphing is such an important skill to learn. It enables children to clearly see information and with that data make obvious conclusions.

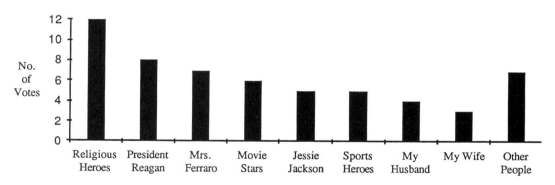

Hero Poll
Question: Who is your favorite hero?

Poll taken at Scotts Valley, California shopping
center by an Evergreen School combination 4th-
5th grade class. (April 1984)

Goal: To be able to graph information from the physical environment and draw conclusions.

Preparation:

1. Colored markers, pencils.

2. Counting items (beads, coins, buttons, cubes, tiles, toothpicks, etc.).

3. 2" x 2" scraps of paper.

4. Standard graph paper (1.7 cm).

Procedure:

1. Discuss with the children what graphing is and how it enables us to record information and then see patterns and relationships in life. Share how almost anything in life can be graphed: height, weight, people who are absent from school, physical fitness events, most popular foods, favorite musicians, monsters, heroes, reading books, hours of TV watching, opinion polls, etc. Graphing skills can range from the simple, such as suggested in step three, to the complex as seen in the "hero" graph on the preceding page.

2. Divide the group into pairs of children.

3. Begin by having each pair graph objects in the immediate room into two groups. Sample groupings could be man-made/natural things, soft things/hard things, brown-haired children/blonde-haired children, fun things/non-fun things, colored/non-colored, etc. Have the pairs of children write each group being graphed on a separate 2" x 2" sheet of paper.

Sample Grouping

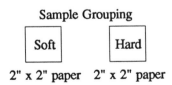

2" x 2" paper   2" x 2" paper

4. Then pass out the counting items to each pair and have the children record what they see by placing a counting item under each grouping.

	Soft	Hard
Piles of	XX	XX
Counting Items	XXX	XXXX

5. When 10 minutes have elapsed, stop the graphing and ask the children to count the items under each heading and write the number on the 2" x 2" piece of paper.

Soft	Hard
5	6

6. Have the children share the results and any concrete conclusions reached.

7. Expand the graphing to include three, four, or five groups (i.e. would you rather go to the beach, park or mountains tomorrow? Is your favorite holiday Christmas, Halloween, Thanksgiving, or Fourth of July?).

8. Hand out the 1.7 cm. graph paper to each child and explain to the children how this lined graph paper is another way of recording information. Instead of writing a group on a 2" x 2" piece of paper, however, this time at the bottom we're going to either write X's or color the group represented in the appropriate columns. Also, instead of using a counting item to record information, we will color in a box above the group heading.

9. Have the children begin with two item groupings on the graph paper and then increase the number to three, four, and five items.

10. Share results and conclusions.

My Body is Like

We can do so many things as a human being. Our rich and varied human experience is created in part by the many talents of the body. In this activity the children will learn to appreciate the human body through the use of analogies. For example, the head becomes analogous to the principal of a school and a steering wheel in a car. The ears become analogous to a counselor in a school and the gauges on a car's dashboard which "listen" to the vehicle's temperature, battery charge, and amount of gasoline. *My Body is Like* will help children understand better the functions of the body parts.

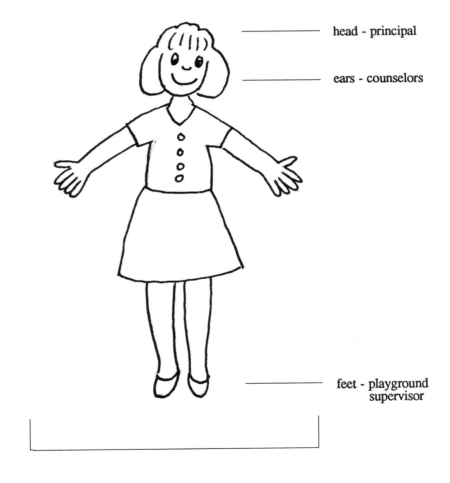

head - principal

ears - counselors

feet - playground
supervisor

Area: Self-Awareness, Vocabulary   **Skill Level:** Grades K-8

Goal: 1. To appreciate and understand the many functions of the human body.

Preparation: 1. Unlined paper, pencils, rulers.

2. Large drawing or picture of a person or unmarked chart paper or blackboard.

3. (Optional) Photocopied or mimeographed sheets of a drawn person.

Procedure: 1. Share with the children how the body has many different parts which serve different functions. In *My Body is Like*, body parts are going to be compared to different things, trying to find similarities. Emphasize that there are no right or wrong answers but that children need to explain their comparisons.

2. Display the large drawing or picture of a person in front of the children. Ask them to compare the parts of the body to different jobs in a school. The head is like a principal, the ears like a counselor, etc. Next compare the parts of the body to the parts of a car. Think of other analogies.

3. Handout unlined paper, pencils and rulers. Ask the children to either draw a picture of a person (big enough to take up most of the sheet of paper) or handout pre-drawn photocopied or mimeographed sheets of paper).

4. Next ask the children to draw lines with a ruler that extend out from the various body parts, labeling the body part. Instruct the children to write along side the body parts analogies from a specific category, like types of animals, types of jobs, colors, etc. For younger children, have them draw pictures next to the body parts.

5. Compare the children's work.

6. Have children trace around each other's bodies on large butcher paper and color in and/or label the body parts.

Chapter 2

SOCIAL LIFE

Social Life

In the absence of any real social education, children tend to take on whatever influence is around them, regardless of merit. Just listen to a conversation between children. Frequently, you'll observe non-listening, defensiveness and, with older children, insincerity. When there is no social education, children learn their social skills by default, picking up habits from their peers or parents or from role models that the media presents.

Learning social skills is immensely important, because we will be with people all of our lives, and our success in life may depend upon how well we are able to communicate and cooperate with others. When we talk about a new social education, we are speaking about the ability to listen, to engage in sincere, meaningful conversation, and also to recognize that there are different levels of relating. There is the superficial, playground level of communication which has its time and place. There is a deeper, heart-felt sharing where there is a greater degree of openness and trust. There are physical ways of relating through touch, and there is a sensitive, non-verbal means of relating which is perhaps the most vulnerable and advanced level of communication.

Getting to Know You

Human relationships are a very important part of our existence. When they are meaningful and rich, we feel very blessed. When they are shallow and uneventful we feel a bit empty and incomplete. Children need to be exposed to different ways of relating to each other so that with this awareness they can choose the type of relations that will most fulfill them.

Goal: To become aware of several different levels of social relationships.

Preparation: Have on hand some juice and other snacks.

Procedure:

1. While eating and drinking some snacks and juice, everyone socializes for five to ten minutes. The amount of time depends on the grade level of children. Encourage everyone to mix and meet with as many others as possible so that the conversation doesn't get too deep but stays at a relatively superficial level.

2. For younger children (K-2) have everyone exchange continental hugs, cheek to cheek, first on one side, then on the other. Continue around until everyone has hugged. Older children can shake hands or bow to one another.

3. Next, have everyone pair off and either sit on the floor or on chairs, knee to knee, facing each other. For approximately fifteen seconds have the pairs look into each other's eyes in silence, becoming aware of that level of communication. Exchange partners several times.

4. Now ask the children to participate in a deeper conversation while still working in pairs. Suggest that each person in a pair answer what things make them happy and what things make them sad. The other partner should listen in silence. Switch roles. If time permits exchange partners.

5. Discuss with the children which activities they liked the best and the least. Explore together the reasons for the different preferences. Finally, ask the children what they want from their relationships. How would they like to be related to?

Sorting and Classifying People*

People are very much alike and yet so different. Those similarities and dissimilarities can cause friendship and alienation alike. In this activity children are going to use an intellectual skill to sort people into different groups based on any one of numerous attributes. By doing this fun activity, children get to know characteristics about themselves better by seeing the characteristics of other children. Children can be grouped in a variety of ways, such as: appearance, likes and dislikes, types of emotion, family, astrological signs, etc. Children love to explore these differences.

Area: Self-Awareness, Vocabulary, Logic   **Skill Level:** Grades K-8

Goal: To determine distinguishing characteristics between children.

Preparation: 1. Paper, pencil (optional). For older children this activity can be recorded on paper.

2. Begin by having the children select two attributes that would divide the group into two parts. Sample groupings are: boy/girl, tall/short, bluejeans/non-bluejeans, dark hair/light hair, etc. Now split the group according to the two attributes.

3. Next have the children add two more distinct attributes that now create four groups altogether: a) boys with brown hair, b) boys with blonde hair, c) girls with brown hair, d) girls with blonde hair. Remember that everyone must fit within a group.

4. Continue to add two attributes each time until you can divide the group no further.

5. For extra practice, have the children think of totally new ways to divide themselves and see where the sorting and classifying branching leads to.

*Adapted from *Mathematics...A Way of Thinking*, Robert Baretta-Lorton (Addison-Wesley,1977), Chapter 13

True Recognition

When our personality shines and sparkles like a glistening crystal, we feel wonderful; we wish that high feeling could go on forever. It is just the opposite, of course, when we feel bad about ourselves because of some blunders we made and are seeing qualities of ourselves that we can't stand. We feel deflated at moments like those and want the miserable experience to go away as soon as possible. But both the high and low experiences are equally part of life and we need to accept ourselves as a whole. We have strengths and weaknesses; children need to learn this truth of life.

Most of the time this person is very happy and does not let very much bother her. Sometimes she makes mountains out of mole hills. She'll get hurt just a little bit and start crying and screaming over hardly anything. Her mood is bad when she is tired or when she hasn't eaten for some time. But during the day she acts happy and lets almost nothing get her mad. Sometimes it seems that she does not care what I think. But maybe she really does care but does not show it. She could improve on showing what she feels but overall she's a pretty nice person because she stays happy and does not let much bother her

Area: Self-Awareness, Writing

Goals:

1. To recognize traits of the personality.

2. To describe personality strengths as well as areas that need improvement.

Preparation:

1. Gather together the names of group or class members in a hat, bowl or box.

2. Writing paper/pencil.

Procedure:

1. Pass the hat, bowl, or box around to all members of the group.

2. Everyone draws the name of another group member in secret.

3. Initially, each person writes down on paper a description of their secret person, portraying their positive qualities. The supervising adult or teacher collects the papers.

4. As each personality description is being read aloud, ask the group to identify who they think is being described.

5. If the children are mature enough, have them redo the activity from the beginning, this time describing positive qualities as well as parts of the personality that may need improvement.

Comment: Emphasize that this is a sensitive activity and that children should be fair and considerate in writing their descriptions. The teacher or supervising adult should omit any descriptions which are offensive before reading them outloud.

Full Length Mirror

Isn't it wonderful when we receive warm, nurturing support from our friends and close ones? Love and caring help to make us feel okay as people and feel motivated to go on in life and reach our potential. The *Full Length Mirror* is an activity that promotes this positive support with children.

Goal:

1. To express positive and constructive comments to fellow children.

2. To receive love and appreciation from other children.

Procedure:

1. Explain to the children the goals of the activity and the importance of expressing genuinely positive feelings towards others.

2. Have the group divide into two lines facing one another. One side becomes the receivers, and the other side becomes the senders. Discuss with the children that criticism is not permitted. Positive comments are the focus.

3. The senders next share one or two positive comments with the receiver facing them. The comments can be about a person's appearance, personality, clothing, or some social quality. Encourage them to have eye contact and emphasize that by looking into each other's eyes, the uniqueness of each other can be seen. The receivers should remain quiet during this period except to say "thank you".

4. After approximately ten to twenty seconds, tell both senders and receivers to rotate one space to the right. Participants at the end of the line (moving in the right direction) switch lines and take on a new role of sender or receiver. Continue the rotation until everyone meets up with their original partner.

Diagram A	4	3	2	1	Senders
	5	6	7	8	Receivers

Everyone rotates to their right

Diagram B	3	2	1	8	Senders
	4	5	6	7	Receivers

Manners and Quirks

At the bus stop an elderly man kept massaging his chin while a young businessman regularly tapped his right foot on the pavement, anxiously waiting for the next bus. Across the street at a restaurant a middle-aged woman kept fluffing up the back of her newly-styled hair, wanting to make sure it remained in its proper place. A creature from another planet might observe how strange and illogical these human quirks are. Yet as odd as they might be, quirks are abundantly a part of the magnificent human experience.

Area: Social Awareness, Self-Awareness   **Skill Level:** Grades 2-8

Goal: To become aware of manners and quirks in self and others.

Preparation: Have on hand some juice and other snacks.

Procedure: 1. Discuss in the group what a quirk is and how people are not usually aware of their own quirks . Include in the discussion verbal and nonverbal habits, such as: saying "um" or "you know", wiping the nose, patting, playing or twisting the hair, rubbing toes, gesturing with fingers, and any other repetitive mannerisms.

2. When the discussion comes to a natural close, prepare for a snack. While everyone is eating and drinking encourage people to silently note any quirks and unique manners of expression. After the eating and drinking is finished have the children share what they observed. This awareness activity can also be carried out during play and work time.

3. Suggest that the children observe manners and quirks during the remainder of the day at school and home. The following day have children share any manners and quirks that they observed.

Interviewing

It would have been his last choice on earth to do, but because it was a class assignment, he had to interview other students. The shy boy was paired with a student who was more aggressive to help serve as a model. Off they went to interview. Yes, it was a trying experience for the shy boy, but he made some headway and surely it wouldn't be his last challenge. He might as well begin facing the challenge now and get practice instead of avoiding contact with others. Interviewing students, friends, parents, and strangers presents a wonderful learning experience for children. Children sometimes struggle to overcome self-consciousness. In the area of communication, children learn how to introduce themselves and how to approach others. When using interviewing in Social Studies they become more objective putting their own personal views aside and hearing a different perspective. And finally, in Math, using the interview process children learn graphing skills and how to record information.

Area: Social Studies, Communication, Math   **Skill Level:** Grades K-8

Goal:

1. To learn interviewing skills.

2. To gain confidence in social interactions other than predictable social settings.

3. To be informed of a wider perspective of opinions beyond our own personal views.

Preparation:

1. Decide in advance the subject of the interview. In the past I have had my school children interview people on a variety of topics, from favorite heroes to election polls to questions on friendship. Try to select a topic which is currently relevant to your educational goals.

2. Having selected an interview topic, create a simple questionnaire from which children can read their questions and record their answers.

3. Target the audience you want the children to interview. It could be children at school or in the local neighborhood, school employees, parents and relations, people at a shopping mall, a nursing home, etc.

4. If you wish to conduct interviews at a place beyond normal walking distance, such as a shopping mall, you will need to arrange transportation for the children.

5. For each child, have several interview sheets, a pencil, and something hard to write on like a book or clipboard.

Procedure:

1. Share with the children the interview project they're about to begin. Tell them that they're going to ask people specific questions and then get specific answers which will be recorded on an interview sheet. Brief them on the possibility that some will feel comfortable interviewing while others might not, and that's OK! You will be there as a supervising adult to assist them in any way possible if they have difficulty.

2. Demonstrate to the group of children an example of how the specific interview might be conducted. "Hi! I'm from Evergreen School. We're doing interviews for a class project. Can I briefly ask you a question?" Instruct the children how to record their answers.

3. Ask for volunteers to conduct several experimental interviews before going out and actually doing interviews.

4. Hand out interview sheets and have children use either hardback books or clipboards on which to write their answers.

5. Send out the interviewers to begin their project. If there are children who are really uncomfortable about the prospect of interviewing, consider pairing them with children more socially confident.

6. Tally results and announce to the children the final outcome.

7. Discuss results with the children.

8. Discuss the interviewing process with the children and what their experience was like.

Mirroring Exercise

A philosophy professor once said to me: "Listening is a monumental problem!" If you don't think so, eavesdrop on several conversations or arguments. Communication must be a two-way street: talking and listening. Both subjects have been neglected in schools and homes. When deeper communication occurs between people, there is a wonderful fulfillment and social connection. Compassion, understanding, and love will follow.

Area: Communication, Social Relations   **Skill Level:** Grades 3-8

Goal:

1. To be able to listen to the verbal and non-verbal messages of another person.

2. To recognize the difficulty in communication and to be aware of that in daily life.

Preparation:

Listening is improved when a person is quiet and receptive. Have the children close their eyes for a short time and be still.

Procedure:

1. Begin by telling the children that communication is a very important skill in life. It enables us to make friends, understand one another, and broaden the mind and intellect. Without good communication, we can be misunderstood and left with uncomfortable feelings.

2. Ask for two volunteers from the group to participate in a communication exercise.

3. Ask one child to listen while the second child answers in four or five sentences the question, "What do you like about your life now and what do you wish you could change?" (A supervising teacher or parent may assist with some sample answers to the question in order to stimulate a response.)

4. After the question has been answered, the volunteer who was listening "mirrors" back or puts into their own words what the original speaker said. Emphasize with the listener that it is important to not just parrot back word for word what the speaker said. The listener should arrive at the basic verbal meaning of the communication plus any feelings that come across.

5. Next ask the speaker if they felt fully heard or listened to. If any points in the mirror were incorrect, ask the speaker to restate them and the listener to "mirror" the missed communication.

6. Reverse roles.

7. Pair everyone up in the group.

Mirroring Exercise   43

8. Give the instructions and set a time limit for reversing roles. This will enable everyone to have the opportunity to share and listen.

Comments: Repeat this activity periodically throughout the year but with a different question to answer each time. Tell the children to observe how well they communicate and listen outside the group experience and to notice the same in other people. Discuss their experience in the group.

Chapter 3

INTELLECT

Intellect

The intellect is a tool that enables us to stand back from a situation and figure things out logically. By analyzing, categorizing, and defining the situation, we can grasp it, control it, and understand it. With the intellect there can be a penetration beyond the appearance of things to the actual facts. If life is like a river in which we're being carried along by the current, the intellect allows us to temporarily dock by the riverside and ask some questions that probe the course being taken: Who, what, where, why, how, and when? In receiving answers to these questions, we can get clarity on how to proceed. Then our course is understood, reducing the probability of errors and problems.

In our society the intellect is highly respected. The ability to organize, to communicate precisely, and to create and follow sequential procedures makes things operate smoothly. Imagine a company president whose job is to look at his business from an overall perspective in order to assess the various needs of the company and prescribe the necessary courses of action. If the organizational plan is not thoroughly thought out, or if communication is not made in a precise, step-by-step fashion, the business plans can dismally fail.

Children, too, face challenges every day. How can they make friends? A toy breaks and needs minor repair, or a school paper is due in one week. An adult can very easily respond to these dilemmas and advise the proper course of action, but these suggestions sometimes inhibit the child's own learning process. Wouldn't it be better to let children find their own solutions? In helping them develop their intellects, we are giving them tools and training which will be helpful not only in the present, but throughout their lives.

Opinion/Observation

How can we educate children to discover what is real in life? Every day children are bombarded with masses of information, opinions and beliefs. At home their parents raise them to think along certain lines. Movies and television portray models of behavior regardless of moral merit. With their peers, children are powerfully affected by group thinking and behavior. To discover what is real, beyond the sways of opinion and prejudice, and to encourage that pursuit as an important value in life, is something dearly precious. In *Opinion/Observation* children learn a fundamental skill of discriminating between what is real and what is an opinion.

"Let me think about that one."

Area: Science, Critical Thinking

Goal: To distinguish between what is observed to be factual and what is opinion.

Preparation: 1.   Have on hand a large picture (approximately 8 1/2" x 11") of a person from a magazine, a poster, or a picture from a personal photograph collection. Try to find a picture that is expressive, because that presents more of a challenge to the observation skills of children.

Procedure: 1.   Share with the children the definitions of opinion and observation. Opinion is expressing a view or judgement about something. Observation is the act of recognizing or noting a fact about something.

2.   Choose an object in the room and make several statements to the group about the object, asking the children after each statement whether what was just said was an opinion or observation. Let the children discuss among themselves any different answers, asking if necessary, any leading questions to direct the conversation. Take a ceiling light as an example:

The light is attached to the ceiling. (Observation)
The light is very ugly. (Opinion)
The light is the best light around. (Opinion)
The light on the ceiling shines brighter than the wall light. (Observation)
The light is dirty. (Observation)

3.   Show the picture now and invite the children's statements about the picture. Notice whether their comments are an opinion or an observation and get them to discuss among themselves the different answers.

4.   Ask for a volunteer from the group of children to be the subject of the opinion/observation statements. Ask the children whether comments about the volunteer's looks, personality, etc., are opinions or observations.

5.   Take a recent incident that happened among some children present and ask for opinion/observation comments about it, as in the above exercise.

6.   Extend this process to other activities. Request that children do the same in their free time, and point out spontaneous examples as they arise.

The Ultimate Kid

Variation: As an optional follow-up activity, have children write ten statements on any topic of their choice. Then have them record on paper whether each of the statements is an opinion or observation.

Flow Chart

Flow charts are fun to design and generally easier to follow than written, linear-style instructions. Because of the visual nature of a flow chart, a child is able to grasp connections between the instructional steps and for the whole process. In this activity children are asked to design a flow chart to explain the steps involved in an activity or process of their own choice.

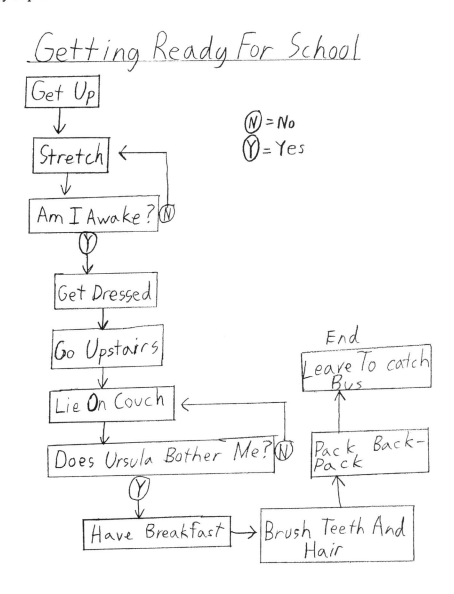

Goal: To describe an activity in a step-by-step manner.

Preparation:

1. Paper, pencil, rulers.

2. Visual diagram of flow chart to serve as a model for the children.

Procedure:

1. Begin by showing a model of a flow chart to the children. Explain how flow charts make the understanding of a process easier because of the visual diagrams and lines leading from diagram to diagram. Each separate task in an activity gets its own box. Alternate tasks can be noted by having dotted lines extending from a box. (See model on previous page.)

2. Ask the children to select an activity from which a flow chart can be made. Require that the activity have at least seven steps included in the flow chart. List some sample activities to serve as examples to the children. Examples: Writing a letter, cooking a meal, replacing a bicycle tire, washing dishes, flying a kite, wrapping a present.

3. Hand out paper, pencil and ruler to each child and ask them to begin the activity.

4. As an extra activity ask the children to color-code their flow chart.

5. When everyone is finished share the results.

I Do Understand You

The art of good communication is a needed skill in all life situations. To some, it comes naturally; others must work to develop it. Giving children an awareness and practice in communication as early and as often as possible will help them in school and in relationships of all kinds. This fun activity will reveal to the children some of the difficulties in communication as well as the need for practice.

One child is instructing another child on how to reconstruct a
duplicate geometric pattern through the use of pattern blocks.

Goal: To realize how accurately we can communicate.

Preparation:

1. Paper and crayons or colored markers for everyone.

2. Cardboard partitions or hardbound 8 1/2 x 11 books that will stand upright, one for every two persons.

Procedure:

1. Everyone draws a simple sketch on plain paper, and keeps it hidden. It can be a geometrical form, a symbol, a nature scene, or still life. The drawing should not be complicated.

2. Have the group pair off, but keep all drawings concealed. Place partitions between each pair.

3. Within each pair, one person will describe his/her drawing. No peeking! The describer will have to formulate his words and thoughts very carefully to convey exactly how and what the partner is to draw. Example: "Draw a square with one inch sides two inches from the left hand corner of the paper."

4. Switch roles.

5. Compare results between the original drawings and the replicas. As a group, share the results and examine the reasons for success or failure and whether the communication was effective.

Variation: Have children build patterns with pattern blocks instead of drawing a picture.

Sorting and Classifying

Everyday we classify life and make distinctions in order to make sense of a wide variety of impressions and information. A busy mother and housewife must arrange her day. A carpenter cuts six pieces of wood in exact precise sizes in order to complete his job. A corporate secretary divides daily mail into half a dozen categories. These examples of real life sorting and classifying activities use various levels of intellectual skill. The following activity challenges children to improve their powers of critical discernment.

Goal: To verbally describe or write descriptions distinguishing an object or child from other objects or children.

Preparation:

1. Have on hand groups of similar objects that can be sorted into numerous categories for every two children (buttons, foreign coins, shells, pebbles, etc.).

2. Paper, pencils

Procedure:

1 Begin by asking the children to verbally classify various objects in the room according to their different attributes. Colors, sizes, shapes, weights, etc. are a few attributes by which objects in a room can be classified.

2. Next begin sorting the objects in the room by selecting attributes that create two distinct groups. Examples are metal/non metal - big/small - heavy/light. Create as many groups as time permits.

3. Now have the children select only one group (such as light/heavy) from which further sorting will take place. Then branch out into four groups, adding another set of attributes to the original two. Below is a model tree or diagram to illustrate the above sorting and classifying process:

<u>Objects in the Room</u>

light in weight   heavy in weight

off floor   on floor   off floor   on floor

Ask the children to see if they can create any further classifications.

4. Now hand out a group of objects to every two children and tell them to sort and classify. Younger children only need to divide the objects into separate piles while older children can write down their groupings according to the model tree shown in step three.

5. Exchange groups of objects and with older kids see if new groups can improve on the efforts of the previous groups.

What If

So often we have worries in our lives that are like computer program loops: they just keep going around and around covering the same territory. We don't necessarily deal with our particular anxiety; instead we dwell on the misfortune that might occur and we feel anxious as a result. Children, being imitators of adult habits, will adapt some of this stress into their lives, too. We can teach children to deal constructively with worry. A simple but effective technique, called "What If", encourages children to examine their anxieties and free themselves of the accompanying fear.

Fear: I have a fear of earthquakes.
Result: Pain that people would go through
People would be unhappy.
Level of joy in universe goes down
The pain would last until people
recover. We got used to it.
We are back where we started.
We go on living.

Area: Self-Awareness, Writing

Skill Level: Grades 3-8

Goal:

To understand how a fear can be resolved.

Preparation:

1. Paper and pencil for everyone.

2. Talk about how people worry in life about big thing and about little things. Ask the children to define what worry is and give examples from their own lives.

3. Share the "What If" technique for lessening worry. Basically, this technique examines a worry by asking "What If" questions. Demonstrate the technique by asking a child to volunteer a fear they're having which can be shared with the rest of the group. Share with the child and the rest of group that fears that are too threatening or too personal shouldn't be expressed unless the person feels absolutely safe and comfortable. Present some examples of fears that children may have: taking tests, making friends, having nightmares, worry over an injured pet, darkness, nervousness over an upcoming birthday, etc. The following dialogue illustrates the method:

Child: I'm worried about the spelling test tomorrow.

Adult: What is it about the test that worries you?

Child: I'm worried that I'll fail.

Adult: What happens if you fail?

Child: Then I'll feel bad and embarrassed.

Adult: What if you feel bad and embarrassed?

Child: Well, then I won't want to be around anybody.

Adult: What happens if you don't want to be around anybody?

Child: Well, then I won't.

Adult: What will happen then?

Child: Then I'll be alone.

Adult: How will that be for you?

Child: I can handle that.

4. Next ask the children to write down several fears on the paper that has just been handed out.

5. After writing down a number of fears and worries, have the children each select the fear that they would most like to rid themselves of at this time.

6. Tell the children to mentally ask themselves "What if" questions with their fear. In other words, what will happen if their fear comes true? What is the worst that can happen? Request that the children write down only the results of what they imagine will happen. (See model on page 59.) The children should continue writing the results of their fears until they see through their fears or reach a comfortable ending.

Love Seat

Whenever we did the *Love Seat* in my classroom, one-third of the class would invariably raise their hands wanting to go first. Kids like this activity because they learn what their classmates and peers like about them plus what might need improving in their character. The *Love Seat* encourages sharing feelings and perceptions in a safe, non-threatening environment. It trains children to give direct and yet very sensitive feedback. If we are to grow and thrive as human beings, we need to be aware of our strengths and equally aware of our areas needing improvement.

Area: Self-Awareness, Communication   **Skill Level**: Grades K-8

Goal:

1. To learn to communicate skillfully and effectively to another person their strengths, and their areas of weakness which need improvement.

Procedure:

1. Form circles of two to ten children. If there are more than ten children, form two circles. It is best to have everyone seated in chairs or on a carpeted floor.

2. Ask for a volunteer to sit in the middle of the circle(s) while everyone else remains on the circle periphery facing the center.

3. One by one, the children on the periphery face the person in the middle and say one positive thing about that person and one item that the person needs to work on. Suggest that the children giving the feedback be still for a few seconds while looking deeply into the eyes of the volunteer. This will guide the participants into a deeper level of perception. The person in the center will quietly listen to all comments except for an optional "thank you".

4. When everyone has finished, the volunteer in the middle says one thing he likes best about himself and one thing he feels he needs to work on.

5. Rotate everyone into the middle of the circle until everyone has had the opportunity to receive feedback. Some groups have one child in the center circle on a daily basis.

6. As an added option, record the feedback on paper and when the activity is finished, distribute the paper to help everyone recall what was said.

Comments: It may be that not everyone will feel comfortable, either in the center of the circle or in giving feedback. Strongly encourage everyone to participate, but never force anyone. This activity can bring children much closer together because of the shared love and honesty. Families also benefit from the *Love Seat's* close communication and intimacy.

Mime

Mime is simply acting out a character or scene by body movement. No speech is used. Children love this activity, especially when they are given a challenging assignment to act out. Mime topics can range from courtroom scenes to factory assembly lines as performed by large groups or simple tasks done by individuals like fixing a flat tire or making a peanut butter and jelly sandwich. Any activity that involves a sequence of events is workable. Imagination, mental planning, and physical coordination are required in the process. In *Mime* all the parts work together like a symphony to produce a magical show.

Goal: To skillfully portray an activity's sequence of events in mime.

Preparation: Think of several scenes, both individual and group, that children can act out. Fixing a flat tire, making a peanut butter and jelly sandwich, lifting weights, etc. are examples of individual mimes. Examples of group mimes are big machines, factory assembly lines, circus performers, and people at a grocery store.

Procedure: 1.   Talk about mime and what it is. Emphasize to the children that the acting is silent and done solely with the body.

                        2.   Demonstrate a mime act in front of the children to familiarize them with the process.

                        3.   Ask for individual volunteers from the group of children to act out a process in mime. If children can't come up with their own ideas to act out, then suggestions should be made by the supervising adult.

                        4.   After trying individual mimes, try a group mime.

                        5.   Talk about the mime experience with the children discussing what worked, what didn't work, and why.

Sequencing

When children first begin to speak, sometimes just a single word communicates a complex perception or need. When their language ability increases the verbal expression is still tenuous but nevertheless understandable. Instead of food they might utter "Eat food!". Eventually in a child's development there comes a time when the information expressed must take on a more intelligible form in order for communication to occur. Language begins to develop a sequential pattern. Sentences and stories have a beginning, middle, and end. Children hear stories read to them, observe the sequence of events around them, and imitate the speech patterns of adults. The following activity helps children practice the skill of sequencing in both speaking and writing.

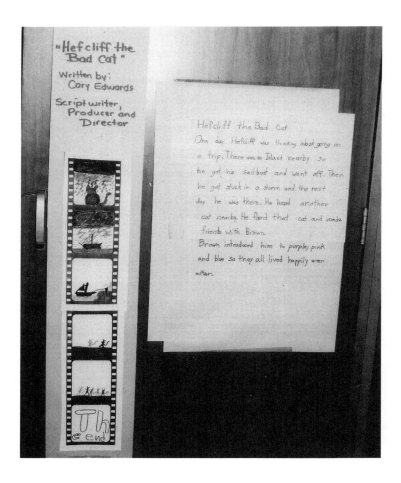

Area: Language, Art, Writing   **Skill Level:** Grades 2-8

Goal: To further develop oral or written language sequencing skills through making a story on film.

Preparation: 1.   Have available blank plastic strips which can be drawn on with permanent felt pens. As an alternative, have available rectangular sheets of 3" x 3" paper strips that are a larger replica of plastic filmstrip frames as the picture on the previous page shows.

2.   For preparing paper strips you will need a ruler, black felt-pen, and an unlined sheet of 8 1/2" x 11" paper. First measure out on your paper side-by-side two 3" x 9" rectangles. Then divide each rectangle into three 3" x 3" frames. Complete the paper strips by drawing in with the black felt-pen the border loops and outlines as shown on the previous page. Xerox each sheet so that every child receives two 3" x 9" paper strip rectangles.

3.   Lined writing paper.

4.   Felt-pens.

5.   Overhead projector/ filmstrip projector.

Procedure: 1.   Place a lined sheet of paper in front of each child and have them write the name of their favorite physical sport or game to play.

2.   Have the children close their eyes and visualize the activity they named. Examples: football, skiing, soccer, jump rope, freeze tag, etc.

Tell them to visualize themselves playing their favorite sport. Encourage them to be playing the best they can. Examples for the visualization script are as follows:

> *"You are doing the best you can...You are enjoying playing this sport*
> *wherever you are, on a playground, in a stadium, swimming pool,*
> *ski slope or any other place...You hear a crowd cheering for you...etc."*

3. After the visualization have the children take the plastic strips or paper strips and draw the sequence of events with felt tip pens. There should be six frames for every child.

4. When the children complete the drawings have them write out the story on lined paper or orally tell the story.

5. If using plastic strips, use the overhead projector to "project" the story. If using paper strips, hold the strips up so that everyone can see. As the drawing is being projected the child will read or tell the sequence of the story.

6. Repeat this activity again but have children think of stories instead which can be drawn onto strips.

Comments: There are commercially made filmstrip rolls which are quite effective either on an overhead projector or used in a filmstrip projector.

Chapter 4

SENSE OF SECURITY/EMOTIONS

In the depths of our heart we will find who we are. Unfortunately, we don't give our hearts enough attention in our lives. We listen much more to the mind or the part of us that is consumed in practical, day-to-day activity. Yet even though we may not pay much attention to the calls of the heart, we are nonetheless moved and motivated by it. We feel insecure about money, possessions, a relationship, or a job and we take steps to remedy the situation. Or the fact that we truly love or care about someone moves us to give them a present or do something nice for them. To grow and mature as people, we must begin exploring and getting to know our hearts. A lot of people increase their mind-skills. Yet even if we do a lot of thinking and try to avoid the feelings, the heart (the feeling self) is who we really are. It is that part of us that is living life.

The development of the heart needs to start with children. Because children are still in touch with their feeling natures, this becomes a ripe time to encourage the sharing and investigation of the heart. A boy has an argument with another boy over possession of a playground ball. What is that boy feeling and why? What is the deeper feeling under the surface feeling. Is there hurt under the anger? This exploration of feelings not only resolves conflict but also brings greater maturity and self-awareness. Instead of ignoring feelings and disregarding them as irrational and unpractical, we need to elicit children's heart-felt responses whenever possible. If we don't give children the opportunity for this self exploration, then the feelings become submerged in the psyche. When they do resurface, those feelings can take the form of subdued aggression, neurosis, or even a hopelessness. Deeper feelings of love, compassion, and even sorrow will in all likelihood fall out of reach of the suppressed individual who will live an empty, barren life as a result. Feelings are natural. They arise in our consciousness for a reason. If we have a pain in our body we quickly attend to it. We need to educate our young to respond to their feeling natures in the same way.

Nature also holds a key in the unfoldment of the heart. Nature gives freely of itself. Apples fall from trees without an asking price. The sun shines its light on the Earth every day and we never see a bill at the end of the month. If we can understand the beauty and radiance of nature, we will in turn reinforce those qualities in ourselves and in our children.

Knowing a Tree as a Friend

Trees can become very special friends. They give us shade in the heat of summer, make great climbing ladders for children, and adorn the environment with varying shades of green. Trees give indiscriminately of themselves to all, saint and criminal alike. The unconditional love of a tree makes them especially popular with children. In the following activity the children will become acquainted with a particular tree.

Area: Nature Awareness, Drawing   **Skill Level:** Grades K-8

Goal: To know a tree as a friend.

Preparation:

1. Unlined paper, pencils, paints or colored markers (optional), something hard to draw on.

2. Blindfolds.

3. *A Tree is Nice* by Janice Udry (Harper and Row).

Procedure:

1. Read to the children the book *A Tree is Nice*.

2. Go outside to an area where there is an abundance of trees.

3. Group children in pairs with one blindfold per pair.

4. Next, have one child in each pair select a tree while accompanied by their partner. Instruct them beforehand to become very familiar with their special tree, knowing its size, shape, texture, and what its leaves are like.

5. Next, have the child who selected the tree go back to a starting point and be blindfolded. The other partner turns the blindfolded child around several times to disorient him or her. Then the seeing partner will accompany the blindfolded partner on a quest to relocate the selected tree. Should the blindfolded partner completely lose course then the seeing partner will help aim the partner in the proper direction. When the blindfolded partner has located the selected tree, instruct the partners to switch roles.

6. Have the children regularly visit their selected tree so that they can become good friends.

7. On another day have the children go back outside and draw their trees in detail. Have paints or colored markers available. Tell the children to take great care in drawing a picture of their friends as they will want to represent the tree well.

Trust Exercise

Trust is knowing that you can place your confidence in someone else's hands without fear of being harmed or taken advantage of. With that trust we can feel safe in expressing and acting naturally without inhibition. A trusting environment is essential for maximum learning to take place. To learn is to leave behind familiar ground and enter into the unknown, a sometimes shaky and unstable territory. The *Trust Exercise* helps build a safe environment for learning.

Area: Social Relations, Friendship   **Skill Level:** Grades K-8

Goal: 1. To get to know each other in a fun and nonthreatening way.

                     2. To encourage caring and sensitivity among children.

Preparation: Have on hand a blindfold, one for every eight people (optional).

Procedure: 1. Have your group form a circle; if there are more than eight children present, form several groups. Huddle close together.

                     2. One person at a time goes into the center of the group and is blindfolded (or keeps their eyes closed). That person is then turned around several times and when ready falls backwards, landing into the waiting hands and arms of the other group members. The person in the middle should keep their body straight so that it is more easily caught. After the group members catch the falling individual, they should gently push the person forward to be caught by other people. The process continues. Each person can be passed around the circle for one or two minutes.

Comments: Emphasize with the children to be gentle and not aggressive. The purpose of this activity is to show our caring and develop trust among each other. Anyone who's rough should be asked to leave the group. With children K-3rd grade several adults are needed in the outer circle to make sure no one is dropped.

Exploring Nature

So often we are preoccupied with activities and forget to see ourselves as part of nature. We think what we are doing is important and we spend most of our time focussing on what we want or need. But human beings are relatively insignificant in the pulsating life and natural rhythms on earth and are even smaller in relation to the wider universe. We can, however, tune into nature and contact the wondrous spirit of nature and the enormous power behind it. Children too can take part in this experience. By listening, feeling, and visualizing different parts of nature, they can discover a peaceful side of themselves.

Area: Nature Awareness, Self-Awareness   **Skill Level:** Grades K-8

Goal: To experience nature from a different point of view.

Preparation: A rock, a green plant, and a small animal, preferably a snail or something of similar size that won't escape.

Procedure: 1.   Everyone goes on an outing to nature. The woods, a pond, the ocean, or even a nearby park are ideal places. Try to locate a place where you will have privacy and not be disturbed by loud noises and conversations.

2.   Begin by sitting quietly together in a circle, listening to the silence and to the sounds of nature. Notice the sights and the scents.

3.   The supervising adult places a large rock in the center of the circle and guides the children in the following visualization with their eyes open:

Everyone imagine that you are sitting inside the rock...What does it feel like to be a rock?..Is it hard, old, cool, vibrating?..The rock is part of the mineral kingdom of nature...When you feel like sharing a few words to describe your experience as a rock, go ahead and speak.

4.   When everyone has had a chance to share about the feelingness of rockness, remove the rock from the center of the circle and place a plant inside instead. Now the supervising adult guides the children in a visualization on becoming a plant:

Now extend your awareness inside the plant...What is it like to be a member of the plant kingdom?..Share what it is like to be a plant.

5. Bring the snail or other living creature in the center of the circle now:

Focus on the member of the animal kingdom now...What do you feel like?..Speak out what it is like to be the creature in the center of the circle...Now hold out your right hand and channel energy to the animal. Stay concentrated and send positive energy out through your right hand to the creature. See if you can draw the animal to you. Notice if there is any response.

Variations:

1. If the site of the nature exploration has different objects than the previous ones mentioned, include those in the visualization.

2. After completing the visualization, have the children draw or write about their experience.

Feelings

People experience feelings every day and yet they really don't listen to them very closely. Either they're too busy to look at them or the feelings run counter to several prevailing self-images in society and therefore seem unacceptable. But feelings are a very normal part of human existence. By examining them we grow and enjoy much richer lives. To experience the tenderness of the human heart is to know the depths of perhaps the greatest fulfillment in life. The expression and exploration of feelings is something that can be incorporated into both the home and school settings. A greater understanding of who we are awaits us in doing so.

"FEELING BADGES"

Preparation:

1. Have available some poster board or large sheets of butcher paper and several large colored markers.

2. White construction paper, colored markers.

3. Scissors, scotch tape.

4. Photographs or magazine pictures of people experiencing different feelings.

Procedure:

1. Begin by showing some photographs and magazine pictures that depict people experiencing different feelings. Encourage the children to talk about the pictures and describe the feelings being expressed. Discuss that we all have those types of feelings even though we may experience them for different reasons.

2. Next, ask the children what are some different feelings they've had lately and what made them feel that way. As they share their feelings, write down the feelings on the poster board or large sheet of butcher paper. Add to this "Feeling Inventory List" each day as children experience new feelings or think of others.

3. Have the children make feeling badges, each badge representing a different feeling. Encourage children to make colorful badges of both positive and negative feelings and to be as specific as possible, not just saying happy and sad. Use the Feeling Inventory List to help stimulate ideas of different feelings. When finished, post the various badges on a bulletin board or wall.

4. On another day, ask the children what they are feeling or have recently felt. After each child shares, have them individually select the badge that best matches their feeling and tape it on their chest. Ask them why they feel that way. Continue on around until all the children have participated.

Energy Awareness

Historically, energy is the name given to the ability to do work. Throughout human development, man has discovered new sources of energy to do his work for him. These include: sunlight, winds, flowing water, horses, firewood, natural gas, coal, gasoline, and the nucleus of the atom. But people can give off energy, too. Within each of us, there is a kind of life force or movement of consciousness. In this activity, children have the opportunity to experience and recognize energy in each other.

Goal:

To recognize and experience energy within all living things.

Procedure:

1. Talk about energy with the children. Ask them what it is and what kinds of energy there are, including energies they experience in people. Tell them they're going to have the opportunity to experience energy in each other.

2. As an option have the children experience exercises from the *Exploring Nature* activity in this chapter.

3. The children should close their eyes and take the palm of one of their hands and hold it about two inches from their face. Ask them if they experience any feelings, sensations, or hot or cold impressions. Next have them move their hands to the top of their head, heart, stomach, etc. Discuss any feelings or sensations that arose.

4. Next have the children put one palm on top of another with about 12" of space between each palm. Pump the hands up and down. Discuss any sensations in the palms.

5. Arrange the children in small circles of four to six each. One child at a time will be a receiver in the center of the circle with palms upturned and eyes closed. The other children, as senders, raise their right palms about eight inches from the receiver's heart. The senders now concentrate with their eyes closed and imagine energy flowing from the top of their heads down through their heart and out through their arms into the heart of the person in the middle of the circle. (If the right arm tires, switch to the left, but keep visualizing the energy flowing.)

6. Before switching roles, senders will ask the receivers what they felt. If may be a warm or cold feeling, a tingle, or a feeling of pressure.

The Power of Caring

If we can learn how to use the power of caring our lives would be transformed greatly. The feeling of caring is not just for the benefit of others but also for ourselves. Applying Isaac Newton's Law, "Every action has an equal and opposite reaction", we can see that what we put out comes back to us. It is so important that children learn this principle from which true friendship and getting along with others comes. If a child projects out heart-felt caring, life mirrors back that feeling. When a child is angry or disturbed, life will reflect back disturbance. By practicing the activities that follow, children can learn how to channel their energy in positive directions.

Goal:

1. To understand how Newton's Law, "Every action has an equal and opposite reaction", applies to children's inner states of consciousness.

2. To practice caring towards others.

Procedure:

1. Discuss Newton's Law and how what we put out comes back to us. Give examples of someone whose anger causes life to mirror back disturbance to that person, and show that when a person expresses caring and friendship, a warm, happy feeling comes back. Draw out examples from the children's own lives.

2. Lead the children in the following visualization on caring or make up your own. Read the script as the children visualize with their eyes closed. Read slowly with pauses so visual images can be adequately formed.

   "Take a deep breath and then slowly exhale. Do it a few more times and relax...Visualize someone who needs help right now, someone who perhaps is having pain or difficulty...They could be a person with whom you had a fight, someone who is sick, or even someone who feels sad and lonely. Realize that that person needs your help...See the face of that person very clearly...Now send that person some warm feelings of caring and love. Send wave after wave of good feeling...As you send caring that person's face begins to light up and smile, that person begins to feel happy. Slowly open your eyes now."

3. Discuss what happened in the children's visualizations and what the children feel like inside as a result.

4. Now do an experiment with a group of children. Tell the children that they're going to do a project that involves caring towards others. The purpose of the experiment is to see if showing caring towards others changes those people's behavior and makes them more friendly and happy. Discuss among the children what are some caring actions that can be shown towards a person. Some typical caring acts are smiling, asking someone to play or participate in an activity, saying something nice, sharing food, etc. Have the children select an individual that they feel needs or deserves some caring. When the moment is right, advise the children to begin to show their caring for that person with as much subtlety as possible so the receiver of the actions doesn't feel singled out or self-conscious.

5. Carry out the caring gestures for a week. Older children can daily observe and share among themselves whether the caring actions made the selected person's behavior more friendly or not. Have a final discussion at the end of the week to decide upon the effectiveness of the experiment.

Variations:

1. Put all the children's names on individual cards and place them in a bowl. Have each child, with their eyes closed, pick a card from the bowl. Tell the children that they have become the Secret Angels for the individuals they selected. For one week the Secret Angels will show caring actions towards their special person keeping their own identity a secret. When the week is over, see if the receivers of the caring actions can guess who their Secret Angel was.

2. For older children arrange a visit to a local hospital or convalescent home where injured or older people are in need of companionship.

3 Select a charity organization which distributes money to destitute children. Through fund-raising or voluntary contributions from your children's families, "adopt" a child. Try to establish regular contact with the child.

Chapter 5

CONCEPTUAL MIND

Conceptual Mind

The mind is a storehouse of everything we have experienced in our lives. From these many life experiences, we have formed concepts and ideas about the way life is. New experiences are then processed through these mental concepts. People with different life experiences in the past will have different versions of reality in the present. Because of this filtering, to go beyond our own narrow experiences and concepts to include the mental worlds of others is a big challenge. To tolerate and understand other points of view that may be just as valid as our own perceived "reality" is to mature. How many of us can truly tolerate and understand other points of view without reacting or becoming defensive?

Too often children grow up in atmosphere of bigotry or narrow-mindedness, which so limits the horizon of what they can see and experience that it is like placing a tourniquet on a child's zeal to grow. Life's many options become restricted, and some of the joy goes out of it. It is a wonderful gift if someone at school or at home can expose children to new ideas and, by talking with them, widen their understanding.

The conceptual part of the mind has its limits, but it also has its own unique virtues. Out of the conceptual mind comes our ideals and our heroic models that can guide and inspire us to make a better world. Every culture has some form of a hero who has demonstrated superior effort in courage, caring for others, or showing the way through difficult times. Children are especially attracted towards heroes.

What we do with our minds and what our minds do with us will shape the quality of our experience of life at every turn. The mind has sometimes been compared to a monkey which climbs all around from vine to vine and rarely settles down. If you're in the middle of a difficult project and your mind keeps wandering to the refrigerator or the television looking for something more pleasurable, obviously you can't get anything done. To discipline the mind to stay focused on whatever is in front of us is to discover the wonderful art of concentration. With concentration we can pursue what we really want in life with a momentum that wins out over the distracting pulls and detours of the mind.

Different Minds

As humans we differ from each other in values, tastes, opinions, and experiences. With children, those differences can create insecurity and trigger antagonisms and competitiveness. Children need to discover that people think and act differently because of unique and diverse background experiences. To be different is okay. In this activity children are going to find out just how different their minds are.

Area: Communication, Values Clarification   **Skill Level:** Grades K-8

Goals:

1. To see how differently we all think.

2. To recognize some of our mind patterns.

Preparation:

Have on hand at least three commonly recognized objects. These would vary according to the children's age level. Examples: an apple, Michael Jackson's picture, dictionary, pencil, crayon, radio, Legos, etc. Keep each object hidden until ready to be shown.

Procedure:

1. Bring out the first object. Place it on a centrally-located table, or pass it around. Ask the children individually to tell how they feel or what they think about the object, expressing one idea only. They should express the first thing which comes to mind.

2. Continue with the second and third objects, asking for the children's reactions.

3. Discuss the responses. Show the children that although their responses may vary tremendously, nevertheless the ideas for each individual are valid even if we disagree.

Elderly Advice

More and more schools across the country are incorporating the help of the elderly, especially as the student-teacher ratios increase in the classrooms. These senior citizens have faced many decisions and lived many experiences which could be valuable to children. This makes the potential for learning and sharing very rich. Rather than feeling discarded and not useful, the seniors are accepted, loved, and challenged by this opportunity to contribute their skills, wisdom, and kindness.

Area: Writing, Problem solving　　　　　　　　**Skill Level:** Grades 3-8

Goals:　　　　　1.　To gather advice from elderly adults

　　　　　　　　　2.　To gain a wider perspective and possible solution to a particular problem.

Preparation:　　　　Paper, Pencils

Procedure:　　1.　Tell the children to write about a particular difficulty or problem they're having in life right now. Request that they give supportive background on the problem. Provide examples beforehand to stimulate children's responses. Typical examples: What do I do if kids tease me at recess time? How can I become a better reader? How can I make more friends?

　　　　　　　2.　After everyone has described a problem area in life, tell the children about the next phase of the assignment. The next phase involves the children's interaction with adults in an advice-seeking capacity. Each child will ask an adult's advice on their particular problem. Suggest that it would be preferable that the adults be elderly (sixty-five years of age or older). That way the children are talking to people who probably have made many decisions in their life and have some advice on what to do and what not to do. Have each child ask at least five adults what advice they could offer for the particular problem. The children should record the responses on paper.

　　　　　　　3.　Have children share with each other what the various responses were. Ask them how they liked the experience and whether they benefited from it or not.

To Be a Hero

Most of us have believed in heroes sometime in our lives. Heroes represent someone's struggle to overcome opposing forces and stand tall and brave. Heroes have qualities that we would like to have. It is very important that we do not let these aspirations die, either in ourselves or in our children, because out of these visions comes the unfolding of our potential. Heroes help give us faith so that, like them, we too can successfully meet our daily challenges. With children it is good to bridge the gap between the ideal and the actual with practical ideas that draw out their own inner hero. Otherwise, children can lose their aspiration towards the heroic, especially during adolescence, when the practical world encroaches on their way of thinking.

Goal:

1. To spark the inner hero in each child.

2. To identify the qualities of heroes.

Preparation:

1. Have available several hero stories which you can read to the children. Besides classical myths like *Epic of Gilgamesh, Jason and the Argonauts,* and *Knights of the Round Table,* there are excellent biographies of Eleanor Roosevelt, Cezar Chavez, and Martin Luther King. Some outstanding fictional hero stories for elementary children: *Sign of the Beaver* by Elizabeth Speare, *Homecoming* by Cynthia Voight; and for primary children: *St. George and the Dragon* by Margaret Hodges, *A Chair for My Mother* by Vera B. Williams, *Miss Rumphius* by Barbara Cooney.

2. Poster board or chalk board.

3. Writing paper, drawing paper, pencils, colored markers or crayons.

4. Collect some newspaper clippings of heroic achievements where individuals have demonstrated outstanding valor.

Procedure:

1. Begin by asking the children to define what is a hero and what are some of the qualities of character that heroes exemplify. Ask them who are some of their favorite heroes.

2. Read some newspaper stories on recent heroic achievements. Ask the children what qualities the particular individual(s) demonstrated in their heroic feat.

3. Have the children conduct a poll on favorite heroes. Tell them to ask their parents, friends, relatives, or neighbors and share the results the following day. Record the results on poster board or on a chalk board.

4. Read a hero story to the children and again ask what qualities of character the hero demonstrates.

5. Next have the children either write a hero story or draw a picture of a hero. Make sure beforehand that the children understand that heroes come in all sizes, shapes, and from all walks of life. Some heroes are big and strong, some are brave, and many are very ordinary people who in some special moment bring out unusual strengths.

6. Finally, have the children set some kind of test for themselves that will challenge their character. The test could last from one half of a day to a week depending on the age and maturity of the children. Tell the children that one quality heroes demonstrate is self-mastery or control over personal weaknesses and now they have the opportunity to test themselves in that way too.

Some tests that children have set for themselves:

*Cutting out television for five days;

*Stopping name-calling;

*For three consecutive days saying hello to classmates in school whom they don't get along with or don't talk to very much;

*Sharing a playground ball with other children during school recess time;

*Refraining from arguing with brothers and sisters for five days.

Mapping the Mind

Mind mapping is a powerful tool in the education of our children. The real strength in mind mapping lies in its integration of the creative right brain processes with the intellectual skills of the left brain. This partnership enables us to more easily organize our thoughts, recall facts better, brainstorm creative ideas, and improve overall study habits. With this visual form of outlining, we can see information and connections between concepts much easier than in a traditional outline. And what's more, it is very fun and creative.

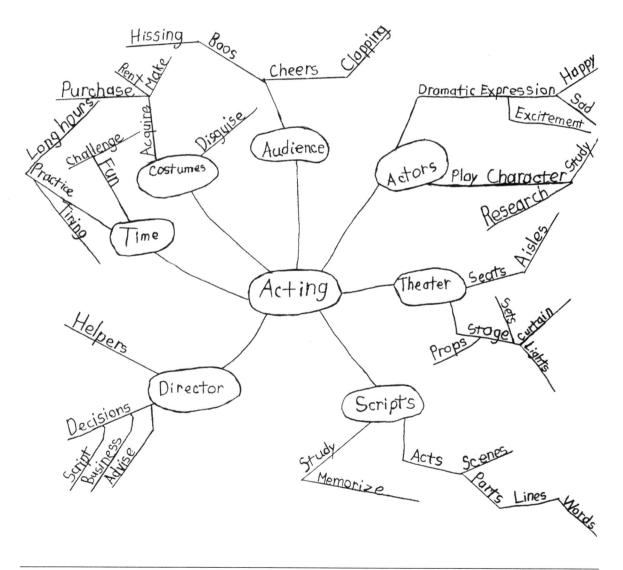

Goal:

1. To use mind mapping as an alternative form of outlining or notetaking.

2. To stimulate problem solving or brainstorming.

Preparation:

Have available unlined paper, pencils, rulers (optional), colored markers and chart paper/felt pens or chalkboard/colored chalk.

Procedure:

1. Introduce the concept "Mind Maps" by drawing one on a chalkboard or poster paper. Begin with a central idea or major topic out of which other ideas or sub-topics radiate out from the middle like rays of the sun. Further branches can be generated from the sub-topics. For each sub-topic and the branches that extend out, use a different color to distinguish that group of ideas from other ones. Conclude the demonstration with the children by pointing out how this form of notetaking and brainstorming can make it easier to learn and remember information.

2. Hand out unlined paper, pencils, colored markers and rulers, if you choose to have the children draw neat lines.

3. Next, instruct the children to print a main topic in the center of their paper, a topic which you have selected ahead of time or have allowed the children to think up for themselves. Ask the children to draw a circle (round or oval) or box (square or rectangle) around the topic.

4. Tell the children to branch out ideas from the main topic and to make further connections or links between the branch ideas, and any new ideas that are related. Each branch and its corresponding ideas extending from the main topic is to be colored differently than the other branches.

5. When finished share the completed mind maps.

6. Consider applying other uses of mind mapping for written reports, creative writing, listing information, problem solving, taking notes, and organizing subject matter.

Variation: For younger children have them draw pictures using the basic "Mind Map" structure.

A picture "Mind Map"

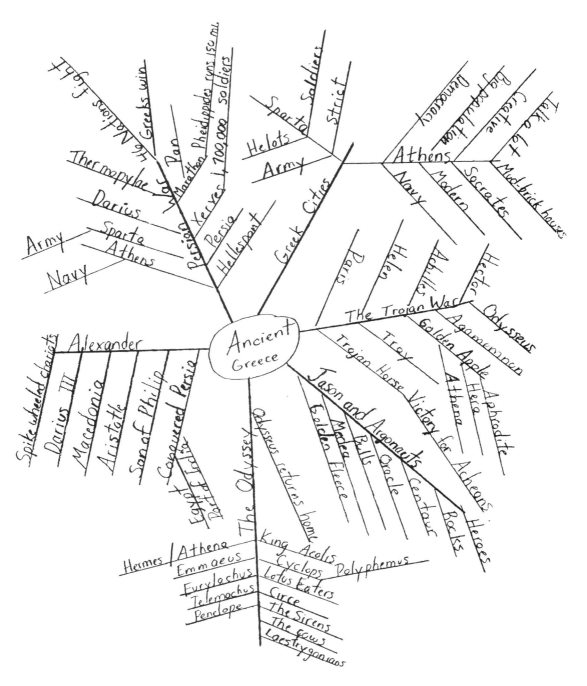

Another form of a written "Mind Map"

Planting the Seed of Poetry

When children are young and their minds fertile like Spring farmlands, it is a great time to plant the seed of poetry. Speaking and memorizing poetry helps build character, develops appropriate speech, and trains the memory. The rhythm of a poem often becomes "catchy" like a song heard on the radio. When the child memorizes and recites a poem aloud, a confidence is instilled because the child feels his own sense of accomplishment towards learning. When the memorized poems are of an inspirational nature, a little gem then becomes a stored treasure in the memory. This provides a natural retrieval system, something to guide and direct us when we've become lost. Just at the moment we need it, a beautiful image or a line of some long-forgotten poem comes floating up from the depths of our mind to lift our spirits or give us a hint about life.

Goal:

1. To train the memory.

2. To learn inspiring poems.

3. To develop appropriate speech patterns.

Preparation:

1. Begin by researching good poetry at a library or book store. Find poems appropriate to the age and interest level of the children you're working with. Below are listed several quality anthologies.

    General:

    Random House Book of Poetry for Children edited by Jack Prelutski, Random House Pub. *Oxford Book of Poetry for Children* Bedrick Press

    Younger Grades:

    Child's Garden of Verse by Robert Louis Stevenson, Putnam and Penguin Pub.

    Older Grades:

    A Galaxy of Verse M. Evans Pub.

    Other Recommendations:

    Old Possum's Book of Practical Cats by T. S. Eliot, Harcourt Brace Pub.

    Visit to William Blake's Inn: (Caldecott and Newbury Award winner) edited by Nancy Willard, Harcourt Brace Pub.

2. Select a poem to begin with and become thoroughly acquainted with it. Know its meaning well and read the poem aloud to yourself several times in your most natural voice.

3. Be prepared to talk about the poem with the children. While there is no one way to introduce a poem, you should find a way that is comfortable to yourself. Know what the theme of the poem is and tie its meaning to the lives of the children.

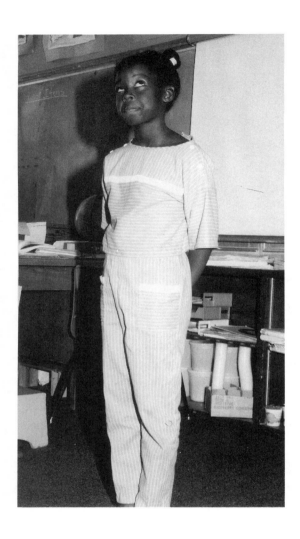

Reciting Poetry

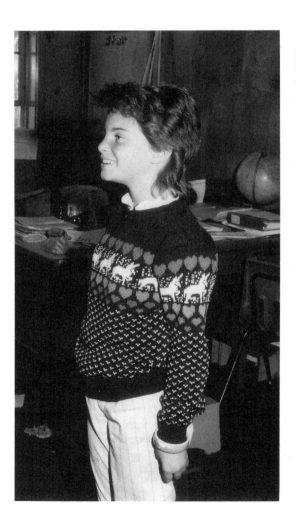

Procedure:

1. Begin by reading the selected poem to the children in your best voice and rhythm. Your model helps set a standard for the children.

2. Discuss the poem with the children, asking them what the poem says to them. If possible find some colorful pictures from magazines or books that visually accompany the poem and help produce an understanding of the poem.

3. Next have the children orally recite the poem along with your guiding voice. Do this several times.

4. For older children pass out a photocopy of the poem so they can become more familiar with it.

5. After each choral recitation of the poem ask for volunteers to orally recite as much of the poem as they can remember. Every day children will observe their progress.

6. Set a date by which children must know the poem by heart. Tell them that they will be expected to recite the poem in front of other children. Stress to the children that clarity of speech, knowledge of the poem, timing, and feeling are important ingredients to have in their presentation.

   For older children points can be awarded on the quality of their presentation, taking into consideration the main ingredients mentioned in the previous paragraph. If appropriate, have the other children who observe each presentation give feedback to the presenter on positive qualities of the presentation and what might need improvement. Stress to the listeners to be fair and sensitive.

Variation:

Have the children write the poem down on paper in their best handwriting or printing. Then have them mount the finished poem on colored construction paper with artistically drawn borders.

Concentration

The mind is a lot like a muscle in that it needs exercise to keep itself alert and productive. Without challenge the mind can become dull and lethargic. The ability to focus on something for an extended period of time is called concentration. The practice of concentration provides clarity in tasks and develops more potential for success. Regardless of people's stations in life, success found in any activity is proportional to the amount of applied concentration.

Goal: To develop the ability to focus for an extended period of time.

Preparation: Candles and matches, a stopwatch or watch with a second hand, and picture or abstract symbol to concentrate on.

Procedure:

1. Talk about concentration with the children and how it is important to develop that skill in order to accomplish something. Athletes, business people, musicians, housewives, car mechanics, secretaries, etc., all need concentration to succeed in their respective fields. Mention how success in school work is greatly helped by one's ability to concentrate.

2. Ask the children to place themselves in a comfortable yet alert position either on a cushion on the floor or on a chair. Encourage straight backs, as slouched backs reinforce undisciplined minds. Request that the children close their eyes and see if they can keep their bodies still without any movement for one minute. Announce the time at the thirty second time interval. Kids love this challenge and in the future will want the time limit extended to two, three, four and five minutes and even longer.

3. As a variation, light a candle and have the children gaze at the candle flame. Ask them while they're concentrating to notice the various shades of color of the flame. After approximately one minute have the children close their eyes and look up into the after-images and see what colors the images are. Repeat the process. Have the children share their experiences.

4. As another variation, post a picture on a wall that is visible to all participants. If you cannot locate a suitable one, create a picture of a circle with a surrounding square and have a dot in the center of the circle for the children to look at. Again have the children gaze at the object of concentration for an extended period of time. Afterwards have them close their eyes and look for after-images.

5. Other concentration activities are listening to one's breath, listening to noises, staring at trees or objects, and mentally reciting inspiring words (like caring or peace).

Chapter 6

INTUITION

Intuition

When we look at the array of potential skills we're capable of developing, the intuition is one of the least recognized or valued. Intangible and hard to measure, intuition is a quiet tool that stands in the background much like a shy person at a party. It knows without knowing how it knows. As a skill, intuition can't be easily verified in a science laboratory. Because of the subjective nature of intuition, we tend to shove it to the background in favor of the more boisterous and rational intellect or mind. Were we able to talk to eminent thinkers like the late Albert Einstein or Henry Kissinger, however, we would get a different picture. These great thinkers acknowledged the use of intuition in some of their insights and crucial international decisions.

The way most of us commonly use intuition in everyday living can be seen in our first impressions of people. We feel a vibration and something about someone turns us on or off. We don't necessarily know why, we just know that's how it is. We all have this power of intuition and use it without knowing we are using it. In fact, many of our decisions can come from hunches, inklings, and non-verbal ways we feel about things.

Intuition comes when the mind is still. Insights and perceptions of reality then appear, filling in the space left by the vacating mind. The tendency in our society, however, is to occupy the mind with as much chatter as possible. TV, radio, gossip, newspaper stories, and fantasy fill the mind to the brim with juicy contents. A consequence is that we lose sensitivity to others and to our own quiet intelligence or intuition. Our ability to make decisions, to see into the future, and to perceive deeper levels of reality becomes impaired. We can do a wonderful service for our children by providing them with the opportunity to further develop their intuitional skills. In doing so, we are equipping them with a tool they can use the rest of their lives.

Supersensing

Have you ever noticed when someone has come into a room and you immediately knew what they were thinking and feeling without having even talked to them? That's an example of intuitive ability. We all have intuitive powers but many of us don't consciously use it because there appears to be no practical value. Were we to listen more closely to our own intuition, however, we would be aided greatly in decisions and social interactions. We would have a sense of what is right without necessarily knowing why our perception is right. The following activity, which trains our intuition or Supersense, has been done successfully by many children. Recently, a Denver TV news station filmed a fourth grade public school class while it was experimenting with *Supersensing* and the results were an incredible 70% accuracy rate!

Area: Communication, Developing Intuition

Skill Level: Grades K-8

Goal: To develop our deeper intuitive intelligence.

Preparation: Intuition is easier to receive when the mind is quiet. Have everyone close their eyes and be still for a short period of time.

Procedure:

1. Have the group pair off with each pair facing one another, knee to knee, either on the floor or on chairs.

2 Each pair holds hands with one person's hands on top (sender) and the other's on the bottom (receiver). Both partners close their eyes to shut out visual distractions.

3. The sender visualizes one thing that means a great deal to him/her: pet, friend, favorite object, etc.. The sender holds this image firmly in his/her mind and sends it to the receiver for approximately one minute.

4. After about a minute has passed, both people open their eyes and the receiver shares the intuitive flashes and images that he/she felt. The sender confirms the accuracy of these impressions.

5. Switch roles.

6. Switch partners.

7. Discuss in the group the results.

Comment: It is best to do this activity with the eyes closed because there are no visual distractions. But for those children that are uncomfortable with their eyes closed, let them keep their eyes open.

Deciding Yes or No

We all have a conscience or a little voice that tells us yes or no when we're about to act or to make a decision. Sometimes that voice gets blurred by too much activity or inner turmoil. But if we listen carefully we can sometimes clearly discern that inner decision maker. The way that inner voice makes itself known differs from person to person. Some people feel disturbed just before they're going to act, indicating that something is "out of tune" about the activity and re-evaluation may be necessary. The ancient Greek philosopher, Socrates, had an inner voice that would only advise when not to do something. We make decisions all day and we pile up reasons justifying an action one way or another. But there is another way, in addition to our rational thinking, to make a decision or take an action. It is important that we train our children to develop their intuition as well as their reason, because intuition is a subtler guide and comes from deeper inside. Its voice is usually more reliable and wiser than the voice of the mind.

Five Yes Or No Decisions

1. Should I go shopping with mom or stay home and bake bread?

2. Should I play with Brynn, build with legos or both?

3. Should I do my spelling work or math work?

4. Should our family move close to Mt. Madonna so I can go to that school?

5. Would I feel happier if I played with Danny or not?

Area: Decision Making, Writing

Skill Level: Grades 3-8

Goal: To facilitate better decision making.

Preparation: Create several hypothetical situations in which the children are faced with having to make a yes or no decision. There are several examples by a ten-year-old boy listed on the previous page which can serve as a model.

Procedure:

1. Talk to the children about how we're frequently faced with difficult decisions in our lives. Sometimes we feel pressure from our friends, family, or society to think and feel a certain way when maybe inside we want something different. Talk about the intuition and how that part of ourself can make deeper yes or no decisions if we listen carefully enough to it.

2. Draw from the children examples from their own lives where they have made yes or no decisions and what were the consequences of their actions.

3. Face the children with several hypothetical situations in which they have to decide yes or no. Ask them to close their eyes before you tell them about the hypothetical situation so they can listen deeper to their inner voice. After each situation is presented ask them what their intuition advised.

4. Give the children an assignment over the next few days to write down five yes or no decisions they had to make, encouraging them to listen to their intuition. Have them share their decisions and the consequences of the decisions, favorable or unfavorable, with the rest of the children.

To Tell The Truth

Intuition enables us to see into the depth of a person or a situation. In this activity the participants will have the opportunity to determine who is telling the truth in a scenario based on the old TV game show, *To Tell The Truth*. Sharp listening, keen perception, and the ability to bluff are key ingredients in this funfilled event.

Goal:

1. To intuitively and logically decipher the accuracy in a person's spoken communication.

2. To become aware that communication is a multi-level process involving not just words but also feelings and subtle vibrations.

Preparation:

Paper, pencils.

Procedure:

1. Have the children write a short one or two paragraph essay on one of the earliest memories they can recall. Tell them to keep their writings confidential.

2. Collect the papers and secretly select one essay that is clearly written.

3. Choose three children from the group, including the author of the selected writing, and instruct them to go to another room or go outside for several minutes, away from the group. There they will read the selected essay together, acquainting themselves fully with any necessary details before reentering the room. The objective of each one of the children is to convince the group that they wrote the essay, and to act in a knowledgeable and genuine way in their responses.

4. Next the supervising adult reads the selected essay to the group so they become more familiar with the story.

5. The group now asks ten questions to the selected three children who are standing in front of the group shoulder to shoulder. If a questioner gets a "yes" response to his or her communication, they may continue to ask probing questions until the person questioned answers "no". When there have been ten "no" responses to ten different children asking questions, then the process stops.

6. A poll is taken to determine which children believe child a, child b, or child c wrote the story.

7. The real author remains standing while the two pretenders sit down.

Seeing Into The Future

Never before have so many people been concerned about the future. Dozens of books from *Future Shock* to *Megatrends* have been written to help us prepare for the many expected future changes. College courses on Futurology are now being offered and conferences happen regularly where information and research on our global future are shared. A lot of the interest arises out of the fast-changing times in which we live. Every aspect of our lives, from family to medicine to business to transportation, has undergone major changes. Understandably then, what we have today won't be the same tomorrow so we'd better prepare for certain anticipated changes. If we do not, we'll be living in a state of uncertainty, knowing that things will change, but not knowing why or how.

Area: Writing, Art

Goal: To develop our intuition and sense of the future.

Preparation:

1. Lined and unlined paper, pencils, colored markers or crayons.

2. A pictorial book on the future. The Hayes/Usborne Company publishes an excellent book on this topic called *Future Cities*.

Procedure:

1. Talk about how much change there is in our lives. New products and new machines are being introduced every day. There are many products around today that weren't invented yet when our parents were in school. Ask the children if they can name some of those inventions (microwave oven, home computer, video tape recorder).

2. Show to the children pictures from a future book and ask for their responses.

3. Lead the children on a visualization into the future. Ask the children to close their eyes and take several deep breaths. Read the following script as the children visualize. Read slowly with pauses so visual images can be adequately formed.

   Imagine if you were able to turn the calendar ahead 1,000 years from today...What would life on planet Earth be like?..What would the houses look like?..What kind of clothes would people wear?..Would the food be any different?...Would there be war, pollution, poor people still?...Try to visualize what the future is like 1,000 years from today... (Take a longer pause than usual)...Now turn back the pages of the calendar until you reach the present time...Feel the ground underneath you...Feel your body...When you're ready open your eyes.

4. Have the children either write a description of what they say in their visualization or draw their imagery on paper. If there is enough time, do both activities.

5. Share the writings and drawings.

Variation: Have the children design new products for the future.

Delphic Oracle

In Ancient Greece when someone had an important question they needed answered they could go to the local oracle who would offer the questioner the appropriate wisdom. The Delphic Oracle was an especially prominent priestess and great leaders, from Socrates to generals, sought out her advice on a variety of questions ranging from who is the wisest person to who will win next week's military battle. In this activity, children have the opportunity to become oracles and enter into a quiet state of mind from which a deeper source of wisdom arises.

Goals:

1. To develop a deeper intuitive understanding of a question or communication.

2. To recognize the value of inner quiet and how from that state of consciousness deeper clarity and wisdom come.

Preparation: Paper, pencils.

Procedure:

1. Brief the children on the purpose of the *Delphic Oracle* and how that ancient way of discovering answers was widely used and respected by the Ancient Greeks. Share with the children that during this activity they must be especially quiet and sensitive, otherwise the oracles won't be able to concentrate as well and let the wisdom speak.

2. Have the children write several questions on the general theme of life from which the oracles will later answer. Examples: What can the Americans do to get along better with the Russians? Will humans ever make contact with outer space aliens?

3. Ask for and select three volunteers from the group who will be oracles. Request that the other children find a seat where they can remain quiet, holding their questions. Tell the children to raise their hands when they want to ask a question to the oracle.

4. Request that the oracles find a very comfortable position, preferably lying down on a carpeted floor, where they can fully relax, or with their heads down on their desks.

5. Tell the oracles that you will lead them into a very relaxed state of mind where their minds will be at rest and empty. Reassure them that this activity will be completely safe, temporary, and somewhat like taking a nap. The oracle exercise will last approximately twelve to twenty minutes.

6. Once the oracles are in a physically comfortable position, verbally guide them through physical relaxation, tensing and relaxing each body part one by one, beginning with the toes and moving all the way up to the head.

7. Next, have the children listen to their breath, hearing the in-breath and out-breath much like the waves of the ocean. Affirm to them that they are becoming very relaxed and calm.

8. When the oracles appear to be relaxed, share with them in a nice soft voice that you're going to count backwards very slowly from ten to one. Each number that is counted will lead them further into deep relaxation. In between several numbers remind them how sleepy they're becoming and how heavy their bodies are. When you call number one, the children should be in a deep state of relaxation.

9. Now begin pointing to the questioners one at a time, who have their hands raised. As the questioners ask their questions, carefully observe the oracles, making sure that they're still in a quiet space. Any sign of restlessness or quick verbal responses to the questions indicates that the oracles are slipping out of their calm state, thus diminishing the sensitive content of the answers. When that happens gradually bring the activity to close.

10. Bring the activity to a close by having the oracles tighten their body muscles and then let go, followed by taking several deep breaths. Gradually request that they open their eyes.

11. Rotate the oracles on another day.

12. For variety have the children write more personal questions that can be answered by the oracles. Example: How can I get along better with my sister? How can I improve my school work?

What Previous Child Oracles Have Said

Questioner: Why are we here on Earth?
Oracle: Nobody is really sure yet. That is a mystery still to be solved.

Questioner: Am I too short?
Oracle: No, you're fine just the way you are.

Questioner: Who am I?
Oracle: A nice person.

Questioner: Why are there nuclear bombs?
Oracle: Scientists invented splitting the atom which makes a lot of power when it explodes. They did it for power.

Chapter 7

IMAGINATION

Imagination

The imagination is clearly the great learning tool of the future. In its infancy of study by brain scientists, psychologists, and to a much lesser degree by educators, the imagination plays a major role in the way we learn and how we perceive reality. Whatever we see in front of us, we are recreating in our imaginations as all incoming sensory input passes signals along the nervous system to our brain. Once the signal enters the brain, we project a replication or image on our mental screen.

The quality of the images we experience will vary greatly depending on how we use our imagination. Left to wander, the imagination becomes a vehicle for fantasy and random thoughts. Without focus or discipline the imagination cannot sustain images or ideas long enough to creatively apply itself to projects. With guidance, however, the imagination becomes a powerful creative force in all endeavors. New directions and visions of reality are created. Intelligent systems of thought arise. These movements of imagery, whether they occur in classrooms, artist studios, business conference rooms, or in family living rooms, have the capacity to create dramatic change in people's lives.

Children's imaginations are already somewhat activated and in many cases are as active as they will ever be in the children's entire lives. Untouched by adult censorship or practical considerations that rule out creativity, children love to bring this exciting faculty into their play and school work. For instance, when asked to draw a timeline of history, many children's urge is to go towards the future where there are no inhibiting models from the past. The uncreated awaits the touch of their imaginations. All sorts of original cars, houses, and spacecraft flow out of their imaginations. In hearing a story you can see by the excitement on children's faces that their imaginations are busily producing animated internal movie pictures to match each sentence that is presented. Whatever the area of learning, whenever the heightened use of the imagination is applied, learning becomes more stimulating and retention of material remarkably improved. The whole education process comes alive.

Visualization

A recent educational conference at the University of Southern California concluded that visualization will be used in every academic sphere by the year 2000! Why would this group of educators and scientists draw that conclusion when visualization isn't used all that much in schools and homes at present? Visualization is primarily a skill of the imagination. By incorporating the use of visual imagery in learning motivation, comprehension, and retention increase dramatically. Learning becomes a multi-leveled, whole brain experience where more faculties of our consciousness are being used. Also, learning is done in a more relaxed atmosphere through visualization. Pretend for just a moment that you are a child faced with the option of reading a two page factual description of the atom and its structure versus being led through a guided visualization where you have a multi-sensory experience of the nucleus and surrounding particles. Clearly, the visualization experience makes the study of the atom a more personal experience which will not be soon forgotten.

Goal:

1. To stimulate the imagination which activates the creative process.

2. To improve listening, comprehension, and retention of facts.

Preparation:

1. To prepare for a visualization, think of a topic or subject currently relevant to the children you're working with. If necessary write out the visualization you'll be leading similar to the one below. For younger children the topic should be simplified and shorter.

2. Lined paper, pencils, drawing paper, markers, crayons.

Procedure:

1. Begin by engaging the children in a Socratic discussion on the visualization topic. Draw out their answers and comments. A pre-visualization discussion stimulates their interest about the topic. Showing pictures related to the topic helps arouse interest too.

2. To help reduce excess physical energy that might distract the children's attention during the visualization, lead the children in several stretching exercises beforehand. Yoga offers many excellent exercises to help relax children.

3. Next, ask the children to close their eyes and relax. Tell them to take four or five slow deep breaths and on the out breath let go of any bad feelings or distracting thoughts.

4. Now begin the visualization using a gentle, soothing voice with adequate spacing between your verbal imagery to allow time for the children's imagination to unfold. If necessary prerecord yourself on a tape recorder to check the quality of your voice before guiding the children.

Flying Like a Bird

Imagine that you are now leaving the room and going outside...You now become a bird, any kind that you would like to be...See yourself as a bird now with your beak, colored feathers, and tiny legs...All of a sudden you take off, flying high up into the air...You see the city you live in grow smaller and smaller as you go higher. People begin to look like ants, trees become little specks of green...You can see so far around you...A feeling of joy and excitement comes over you as you begin to coast in the air, effortlessly maneuvering to the left, to the right, and up and down...It is a great joy to fly. Fly wherever you would like to go...Now you decide to go back down to Earth and gradually descend through the air...You feel yourself flying down, down closer to the earth...The people, trees, and houses below become larger... Finally you land on the ground and turn back into your normal human size... You wiggle your fingers and toes and shake out any loose feathers... When you're ready to, open your eyes.

5. After the visualization engage the children in a creative process. Drawing or painting what they just experienced in the visualization is a great creative outlet. Writing can also be a wonderful expression for the children's creativity. Minimally, have the children verbally share their experiences.

6. Use the visualization process again in whatever topic or area you are studying with the children.

The Sea Hawk

Black slime sliding down
        slippery slimy rocks
Silent sighs soared softly
        in on the breeze
So softly did the Hobbits sound
That we need to hold our breath.
Soaring on the soft breeze
        we had to sigh
From the silent sea
        came a Sea Hawk

                Ian   Age 9

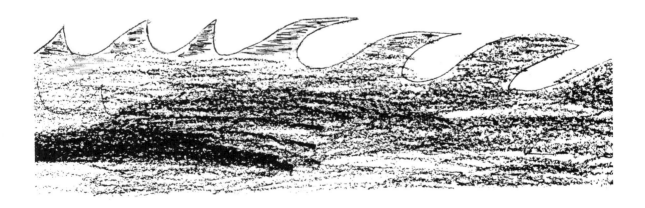

Tapping Creativity Together

We're all connected to one another and the environment in spite of individual and cultural differences. We breathe the same air, eat similar food, inhabit the same planet, and ultimately have the same origins. Many of our ideas arise out of discussions with other people, books we've read, TV shows we've seen, or even if we originated the idea, chances are it has been thought of before in human history. In *Tapping Creativity Together*, children will be encouraged to express themselves artistically together and connect their drawings to some aspect of the nearest friend's or classmate's work. This activity is a cooperative venture in creativity.

Area: Art, Social Cooperation   **Skill Level**: Grades K-8

Goal:

1. To draw something related to the drawing of the nearest person.

2. To understand relationships and connectedness between all of us in the human race.

Preparation:

Have available large sheets of butcher paper for every six to eight children or 8 1/2" x 11" single sheets of plain paper, markers, paints or crayons.

Procedure:

1. Talk about how we're all connected to each other in some way. We get our food and clothing from the same places, we breathe the same air, we enjoy some of the same things and our ideas often come from the same source. We can't live without each other.

2. Now everyone does a group collage together. Everyone must draw something related to the drawing of person(s) next to them. For example, if someone draws a tree, their neighbor might draw a monkey swinging from another tree towards their tree, and the neighbor on the other side may decide to draw a forest of trees with a castle. The purpose is to keep the collage linked together as an expression of wholeness.

Comment: If using individual 8 1/2" x 11" sheets of plain paper instead of large butcher paper, still have the assignment connecting the drawing topics together.

Solving Problems

The National Council of Teachers of Mathematics recommended in a 1980 publication that "problem solving be the focus of school mathematics in the 1980's". Simply learning computational skills or any academic material that is isolated from real-life application won't help us in meeting the day-to-day, unexpected challenges of life. Our education must prepare us to face a full range of problems, routine as well as unexpected. Sometimes when we are faced with a problem we don't know what to do. Our training has taught us to deal with problems very abstractly. Often these problems are too abstract for us to truly understand. Varying the process by which we attempt to solve problems will give us a wider dimension in our solutions. Imagination can play an important role here. To let go of what we think we know and to let our imaginations arrive at a variety of uncensored solutions is to tap creativity. To probe, to question, to experiment, to estimate, to explore, to suggest possible explanations all aim towards strategies which resolve problems.

Goal:

1. To encourage open-ended problem solving by telling, writing, or drawing a solution.

2. To encourage creative responses to problems of a diverse nature.

Preparation:

1. Have available a tape recorder and a tape of soft background music. (I recommend Steven Halpern's *Comfort Zone.*)

2. Paper, pencils, felt pens or crayons.

Procedure:

Part A of *Solving Problems* presents an experimental model to the children showing them how to use their imaginations to creatively work on challenging problem. Part B involves children of third grade age and older who are ready to begin structured problem-solving activities.

Part A:

1. Play soft background music.

2. Ask the children to close their eyes and take a deep breath.

3. Read the following script as the children visualize. Read slowly with pauses so visual images can be adequately formed.

   "You are walking down a path on a very clear day...You are relaxed and comfortable...You see many things on your way and smell the fresh clean air...Soon, you come to a very large pond...You see the other side...You notice there is no way to cross over to the other side...Look around you... What do you see...You need to cross over the pond to the other side... How will you get to the other side?"

4. Ask the children to slowly open their eyes and take a deep breath, ready and alert to solve the problem.

5. Give each child a blank sheet of paper and tell them to draw a picture of how they will solve the problem.

6. After the picture is drawn, have the child share how they solved the problem. Other options are to have older children write down their solutions (younger children can have their responses written down on paper by supervising adults) or have children speak into a tape recorder.

___

Part B:

1. Begin by explaining to the children that every day we face challenges to which we don't always know how to respond. We want to have a close friend but we don't know how to make one. We're trying to fly a kite but for some reason it won't go up in the air. Or we need a certain amount of money for mother's birthday present but we don't know how to get it. Before we can arrive at a solution we may need to understand the problem better. That means asking questions and probing other people to check out their perception of the situation.

2   Next, share with the children that they are going to embark on a problem solving mission. Each child will have a problem or problems to solve. They can create their own problems or draw from a list of suggestions. (See following page for suggestions.)

3. Each supervising adult must set his or her own standards or guidelines for these problem solving projects because each learning situation is unique. However, some guidelines and a recommended step-by-step procedure for each child have been provided below.

Recommended Steps for Problem Solving Project

Have each child do the following:

a. Choose a problem solving project

b. Select materials required

c. Create step-by-step procedure for specific project

d. Estimate time of project's completion

e. Carry out project

f. Arrive at conclusion

Guidelines

*   It is very important in problem solving that children have an opportunity to use their imaginations, letting images freely surface in their mind. Visualization is a great technique for activating the imagination.

___

*   Children need to accept responsibility for their own actions and to know that answers can come from themselves and not from the supervising adult.

*   Their friends and the supervising adult can be resources for ideas too.

*   Children work at different paces. If a child completes a project, he or she should begin another problem solving quest.

*   The problems can cover any topic from math to science to people to sports to music, etc.

*   It is recommended that each child's investigation be carried out in a universal format or procedure so that there is a common understanding and intelligibility in approaches.

Problem Solving Challenges

*   What is the most common source of physical pain? Emotional pain?

*   What is the square footage of the room you're in? The building?

*   What is the total cubic footage of the room you're in? The building?

*   Draw a flow chart of the water in your house showing where it originates and where it eventually ends up.

*   Draw a flow chart of the gas or electricity in your house showing where it originates and where it eventually ends up.

*   Trace the journey of the Sun each day.

*   Which paper airplanes fly best?

*   Which cars have the best gas mileage? Which ones have the worst? Why?

*   How much time do you spend watching TV a day? A week? A month? A year? A lifetime?

*   Create ten solutions on how to deal with a bully.

*   Which people are most or least popular? Why?

*   What is the best way to deal with someone who is lying? Cheating? Stealing?

Wondering at Mythology

Children are deeply engaged by mythology because its stories confirm their sense of wonder at the world. Larger-than-life beings perform miracles that defy the normal order of things, heroes experience adventure and challenging tests of character and courage, and the great mysteries of life are frequently explained in magical terms. Whereas the plot of the average television program will explain life in everyday, mundane language, mythology draws our attention to the heightened human experiences and aspirations, towards the infinite. Stories like Homer's *Iliad and Odyssey*, the *Epic of Gilgamesh*, *Norse Myths*, and countless other tales fire the child's imagination to see possibilities and grasp meanings of the grand order of life.

The Trojan Horse sacking Troy

Area: Oral Listening, Art, Pictorial Note Taking   **Skill Level:** Grades K-8

Goal:

1. To acquaint children with mythology.

2. To retell the sequence of the myth presented.

Preparation:

1. Unlined paper (8 1/2" x 11" or 11" x 17").

2. Pencils, colored markers or crayons.

3. *Taking Notes Through Pictures* squares and lined school paper (optional).

Procedure:

1. Select one of the great mythological stories from history. It is recommended by Henry Barnes in "History Through the Grades", *Introduction to Waldorf Education: Curriculum and Methods** that certain stories are more appropriate for age character of a child than others. Below are his recommendations.

   Grades: K-2   Fairy Tales, Grimm Fairy Tales;

   3   Old Testament Stories;

   4   Nordic, Celtic and Germanic sagas;

   5   Myths of India, Persia, Egypt, Greece;

   Note: The same exercise can be done with history, using:

   6   Greek, Roman history;

   7   Renaissance, Medieval Times, Reformation, U.S. History;

   8   Modern Europe, U.S. History

2. If you are using the "picture note taking" method pass the squares out and instruct the children how to use them (See *Taking Notes Through Pictures* for further instructions).

3. Choose either to read or orally re-tell your selected story. It is preferable to tell the story from memory because a more personal relationship is established between the children and yourself. As an alternative, lead the children on a visualization through an episode of the mythology story prior to artistic expression.

4. Hand out colored markers or crayons, pencils, and unlined paper with which children are to draw pictures representing scenes from the story just told. Recommend to the children as many as five story scenes that can be drawn. (*Taking Notes Through Pictures* can be done at this time.)

5. Continue the process on other days if time permits, collecting numerous drawings and mounting them on a wall.

6. Culminate the mythology story by having the children orally retell the story through their pictures, play-act the story line, or for older children, writing the story in their own words.

Introduction to Waldorf Education: Curriculum and Methods, edited by Earl Ogletree, University Press America

Taking Notes Through Pictures

The mind is far more capable than we normally think and one of the biggest supporting reasons for that statement is the remarkable power of the imagination. Located in the frontal lobe region of the brain, the imagination can heighten our learning because of its potent visual/imagery ability. Research has consistently demonstrated that we learn and recall visual information better than we do verbal information. One very effective visual learning strategy is *Taking Notes Through Pictures*. While participating in oral reading, oral discussion, lecturing, or self-directed instruction, a child draws pictures representing the incoming information. By integrating the verbal and visual modes of learning, there is a far greater retention of the material covered.

Area: Study Habits, Notetaking, Art

Goals:

1. To increase reading comprehension.

2. To increase retention of information.

3. To increase oral or written sequencing skills for language or reading.

Preparation:

1. Have available pencils and "picture note taking" squares. (See previous page for model).

2. Colored markers or crayons (optional).

Procedure:

1. Select appropriate reading material to be read to the students. The material can be a story, history, science, or any other reading material that is vivid enough to spark strong visual images. Length of the activity should vary according to age level: younger children five to ten minutes and older children ten to fifteen minutes.

2. Handout blank paper that has been divided into rectangular squares of three, six eight,or twelve parts, depending on length of the material and age level of children.

3. Tell the children that you are going to be reading some material. While you are reading they should take notes by drawing what they hear. Compare *Taking Notes Through Pictures* to comic strips and demonstrate a model if desired.

4. After the reading is finished, ask the children to complete their drawings, using colored markers or crayons if time permits.

5. As a follow up activity have the children use their "picture note taking" to retell the story. This can be done orally or by writing the story.

Letting Music Provoke the Imagination

Music is a great communicator. Its mere presence evokes certain moods, images, and feelings. The pleasant background music in the dentist's office tells us to relax. Our tooth operation is nothing to take great notice of. At the football stadium the rallying music of the marching band excites us to cheer our team. Or our heart begins to beat faster and our passions are aroused as violin music plays during a romantic movie scene. Music can touch us in very deep ways. The following activity uses music to trigger the imaginations of children.

Area: Music Appreciation, Writing, Art, Vocabulary, Drama   **Skill Level:** Grades K-8

Goal: To stimulate the imagination from a variety of taped musical pieces.

Preparation:

1. Four to six classical musical selections on cassette tape or record, each piece showing a distinct harmony which would create strong visual images. Suggestions: Vivaldi's "Four Seasons", Beethoven's "Ninth Symphony", R. Strauss' "Also Spoke Zarathastra", J. Strauss' "The Blue Danube", Mahler's "Symphony No. 5", Tchaikovsky's "Romeo and Juliet", Tchaikovsky's "Nutcracker Suite", Rossini's "William Tell Overture", Wagner's "Ride of the Valkyries".

2. Writing paper, drawing paper, pencil, colored markers or crayons.

3. Tape recorder or record player.

Procedure:

1. Have the children close their eyes and tell them that they're going to listen to some short musical selections. Ask them to watch what imagery surfaces in their imaginations.

2. After each musical selection is played, either have the children write down in paragraph form or draw a picture of what they saw and experienced during the musical performance.

3. Follow-up activities:

   a. Orally read in class samples of the various descriptions. Show the pictures and talk about them.

   b. Have the children dramatically act out a skit that portrays a theme or feeling from a specific musical piece.

Dreaming

Dreams enter into most of our lives at night, surfacing from our unconscious, and then disappearing when we awake the next morning. That mysterious elusive quality of dreams plus the strange plots involved make dreams very appealing to children. They love to discuss, explore, and act out their dreams. Unknown to themselves, what they are really doing is indirectly facing their unconscious problems that usually get buried in the stream of daily activity flowing through their conscious lives.

Joyful Flight

I once had a dream. I was a little bird and I lived with my brother and sister. One day I woke up and neither my brother nor my sister were there. I searched but couldn't find them. Then I realized that I could still be happy. I flew way up, filled with immense joy and peace. I saw the trees and the flowers, people and buildings, feeling very happy. Suddenly I saw them. We were all very happy to be together again and together we flew on into the sunset.

Area: Self-Awareness, Drama

Goal:

1. To consciously bring dreams to awareness.

2. To act out and re-express dreams.

3. To resolve any problems in a dream.

Preparation:

1. In advance of this activity, ask the children to try and recall a dream(s). Suggest to older children that they have a pad of paper and pencil at their bedside to record any dreams being experienced just as they awake.

2. Lined paper, pencil.

Procedure:

1. Talk about dreams with the children and how by dreaming at night we can let our minds and hearts relax by letting them act out stories. Some of the stories are funny and some are scary depending on what is going on in our personal lives.

2. For younger children, have them briefly share a dream they experienced. For older children, have them write a paragraph (in as much detail as possible) describing a recent yet significant dream.

3. From the various dreams shared or written about, select a couple of dreams that are dramatic and capable of involving a lot of children to act them out.

4. Choose one of the selected dreams to begin the playacting with. Have the child who experienced the dream retell the dream so everyone is acquainted with all the details.

5. Next, have the child who experienced the dream act as director and select a cast to act out the various roles. For younger children, the supervising adult will have to lend some assistance here.

6. Before acting out the dream, ask the director if he/she would like to change the dream in any way and end on a happier note (a technique developed by the Senoi tribe in working with their own children). The director will indicate here whether he/she wants to or not and if so what the various actors should do.

7. Now begin the play-acting of the dream and watch the action unfold!

8. Act out other dreams, making sure as many people who haven't had a chance to participate do so.

9. Discuss and share among yourselves what happened.

BOOKS, CASSETTES AND WORKSHOPS

OTHER BOOKS FOR EDUCATORS AND PARENTS

AVAILABLE FROM

UNIVERSITY OF THE TREES PRESS

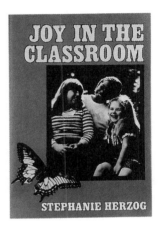

Joy in the Classroom   by Stephanie Herzog

This is a heartwarming, personal account of Stephanie Herzog's experiences teaching "centering", awareness games and conflict resolution to public school children. A veteran teacher, Herzog shares a simple but powerful process that produces amazing breakthroughs in children. Watch children grow in receptivity, caring for others, self-discipline, creativity and inner stability.

224 pages $7.95

Meditating with Children: The Art of Concentration and Centering   by Deborah Rozman, Ph.D.

Wouldn't you like children to be more attentive and creative? This handbook is for parents and teachers who can use meditation as a way of developing concentration and creative imagination. Studies have shown that meditation will: improve concentration, reduce hyperactivity, encourage self-discipline and release boundless creativity.

Fifth printing   160 pages $7.95

Meditation for Children   by Deborah Rozman, Ph.D.

Written especially for parents and families that want to evolve together with their children. You can help your child and your whole family relate to life with new joy through the miracle of meditation.

160 pages $6.95

Creative Conflict by Christopher Hills, Ph.D.

A process to help resolve conflicts between children or adults which really works. Seven steps to real listening and communication. A must for every classroom.

324 pages $7.95

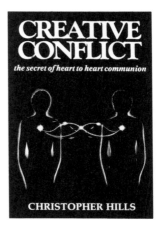

How to Recharge Your Brain by Christopher Hills, Ph.D.

This method of recharging your total brain with bioelectricity and sustaining life energies for perfect health has been used by great human beings throughout history. In this revolutionary new approach to revitalize your brain you will learn new facts about left brain/right brain functions. The workbook provides space for you to chart your progress as you recharge your brain. A tape for easy listening by the author explains how to recharge each area of brain. By developing your power to trigger brain hormones you can experience heightened awareness of your brain potentials.

Workbook and cassette tape $14.95

Rise of the Phoenix by Christopher Hills, Ph.D.

Dr. Hills shares his breakthrough research into the human brain, showing us how our seven brains evolved over the ages and how they correspond to seven distinct levels of consciousness. He explains why the next step in the evolution of society depends on the awakening of the higher brain functions in each one of us, because our personal growth and the evolution of society are identical and inseparable. He shows that if you want a new world, with peace, freedom from hunger, economic security and resolution of conflict, then you have the power and the instrument within you to bring it all about.

1024 pages $24.95

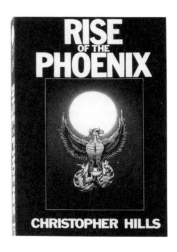

NEW CASSETTE TAPES

How to Build Self-Esteem in Children by Jeffrey Goelitz

A child's ability to learn is closely tied to his/her self-esteem. This tape will show you how to build your child's self-concept through specific techniques and strategies. Discover seven ways to improve communication and how to reinforce a child's strengths while refining their weaknesses. You'll take away a realistic, workable program which will greatly improve the quality of your child's life.

Sixty minute cassette $9.95

How to Resolve Conflict with Children by Jeffrey Goelitz

Children live in an increasingly high-pressured world which adds conflict to their family and social lives. We can help them best by teaching communication and how to get along with others. You will learn simple but very effective methods which help children resolve conflict. Discover four basic questions to ask yourself when facing conflict with children. Children will grow as "peacemakers" and learn to express their feelings constructively.

Sixty minute cassette $9.95

Meditating with Children by Deborah Rozman, Ph.D.

Learn how to teach children the great art/science of meditation using Dr. Rozman's five-step method. Author Rozman narrates a selection of delightful meditations from her book, including the favorites: "Spaceship Meditation", "White Light Meditation", "Balloon Meditation". Her calm, soothing voice helps to take you into quiet states of heightened awareness. Can be used with the gifted, retarded, average or hyperactive child, as it opens untapped areas of the brain. For children of all ages. (Adults love them, too!)

Sixty minute cassette $9.95

Joy in the Classroom by Stephanie Herzog

This charming tape, recorded live in the classroom, can revolutionize the atmosphere in your home or classroom. Stephanie Herzog, author of the book "Joy in the Classroom" shows how to lead the children through delightful centering exercises which children love. Come glide on a rainbow! Break forth from a cocoon into glorious flight as a butterfly. Eight years of research in public and private schools show that these exercises bring marvelous changes in children. Start now and watch your children grow. For children ages five to eleven.

Sixty minute cassette $9.95

WORKSHOPS

THE ULTIMATE KID

"The Ultimate Kid" workshop is for all parents and teachers who want to bring the most out of their children. Based on the latest learning theories in brain research, seven critical areas of a child's development are addressed to create a whole, balanced education. Forty-five practical activities are offered in a step-by-step instructional format that trains children to develop their sensory, social, intellectual, emotional, conceptual, intuitive and imaginative capacities. Children will learn:

- Mind-mapping
- Picture-Note-Taking
- Sorting and Classifying Objects
- How to Deal with Feelings

- Visualization
- Problem Solving
- Mime
- Interviewing

- Many other Skills and Activities

HOW TO BUILD SELF-ESTEEM IN CHILDREN

Do you want to build your child's self-esteem? Is communication with your child in need of improvement? Do you want to unfold more of your child's potential? In this workshop you will learn:

- How self-concept is developed in children
- How your relationship with your child contributes to building self-esteem
- Seven ways to improve communication with children
- How joy and caring blend together to build self-esteem
- Ways of reinforcing a child's strengths and refining their areas of weakness

HOW TO RESOLVE CONFLICT WITH CHILDREN

Our children live in an increasingly high-pressured world. Consequently, conflict and stress often infringe upon families and the ability of its members to relate to one another. This workshop will present you with several simple but very effective methods which help children and parents resolve conflict. These methods have been used successfully in homes and schools to help children work out conflicts and stop on-going fights. In this informative and experiential workshop you will learn:

- Four proven methods to resolve conflict

- How to help children develop peace-making skills

- How to teach children to express feelings constructively

- What escalates conflict versus what de-escalates conflict

- Four critical factors to consider when facing a conflict with children

- How to resolve conflicts with students, siblings, neighborhood kids, parents, and teachers

To further inquire about these workshops write:

Jeffrey Goelitz
P.O. Box 527
Boulder Creek, CA
95006

UNIVERSITY OF THE TREES PRESS
P. O. BOX 66, BOULDER CREEK, CA 95006

BOOKS AND TAPES OF SCIENCE AND SPIRIT

ORDERED BY:
(please print)

NAME _____
ADDRESS _____
CITY ___ _____
STATE _____ ZIP _____
Home phone # ( ) _____
Office phone # ( ) _____

For Faster Service
Charge Card Users Call TOLL-FREE

1-800-372-3100
(in California call 1-800-423-5784)
Please call between 9am and 5pm
(Pacific time) Monday thru Friday

Item #	Qty.	Item Description	Price	Amount

POSTAGE & HANDLING (CHECK ONE)
- ☐ U.S. Mail (book rate). $1.50 for first item; $.45 for each additional item.
- ☐ UPS. $2.50 for first item; $.50 for each additional item.

Foreign orders see Foreign Shipping Schedule.

SUBTOTAL
P&H
Air (add 7.00)
Sales Tax 6¼ % (CA residents)
TOTAL

PAYMENT OPTIONS:
Please charge my credit card (checked below)
☐ MC   ☐ VISA   ☐ AM EX
☐ Check or money order enclosed
(payable to "UTP") Sorry, no C.O.D.'s

Expiration Date [mo.] [yr.]

Credit Card Number [ ][ ][ ][ ][ ][ ][ ][ ][ ][ ][ ][ ][ ][ ]

Signature X_____

GIFT ORDERS If part of your order is to be sent as a gift to someone else, fill in the following information and we will mail it for you.

ITEM(S) _____
SEND TO: _____
ADDRESS _____
CITY _____ STATE _____ ZIP _____
PHONE ( ) _____

Item#	Book Description	Price	Item#	Cassette Description	Price
1070	Joy in the Classroom	7.95	3410	How to Build Self-Esteem in Children	9.95
1080	Meditating with Classroom	7.95	3411	How to Resolve Conflict with Children	9.95
1085	Meditation for Children	6.95	3140	Meditating with Children	9.95
1005	Creative Conflict	6.95	3130	Joy in the Classroom	9.95
3407	How to Recharge Your Brain	-	-	Workbook and Cassette	14.95
1115	Rise of the Phoenix	24.95			